Exponents

Name _____

Write in exponential notation.

1. 5 x 5 x 5 x 5 x 5 _____

2. 3•3•3•3•3•3•3 _____

3. 11•11•11•11 _____

4. 9•9•9•9•9•9 _____

5. 2•2•2•2•2•2•2•2 _____

6. 3.8 x 3.8 _____

7. 14•14•14 _____

8. 4 x 4 x 4 x 4 x 4 _____

9. 100•100 _____

10. 4.5 x 4.5 x 4.5 x 4.5 _____

11. (0.7)(0.7)(0.7) _____

12. 6•6•6•6•6•6 _____

Write the numeral.

13. 12^2 _____

14. 21^1 _____

15. 2^8 _____

16. 3^5 _____

17. 20^3 _____

18. 4^3 _____

19. 21^2 _____

20. 15^2 _____

21. 5^4 _____

22. 7^3 _____

23. 2^6 _____

24. 9^2 _____

25. 2^7 _____

26. 8^3 _____

27. 3^4 _____

28. 18^2 _____

29. 33^1 _____

30. 15^0 _____

31. 6^3 _____

32. 2^5 _____

33. 50^1 _____

Exponents

Name _____

What did the duck say to the cashier?

To find out, locate the answers to the following problems at the bottom of the page. Put the letter of the problem above the corresponding answer.

L. $4^2 \cdot 4^3$

O. $12^{20} \div 12^{18}$

I. $(2.1)^{13} \div (2.1)^{11}$

U. $(9.04)^9 \div (9.04)^8$

Y. $2^3 \cdot 2^4$

P. $10^2 \cdot 10^2$

B. $5^{16} \div 5^{12}$

I. $(6.6)^{10} \div (6.6)^8$

M. $7^{17} \div 7^{14}$

S. $3^4 \times 3^2$

T. $(9.9)^1 \cdot (9.9)^1$

N. $(0.1)^3 \times (0.1)^1$

H. $8^{11} \div 8^8$

L. $(0.11)^8 \div (0.11)^8$

T. $(0.3)^2 \cdot (0.3)^1$

10,000	9.04	98.01		0.027	512	43.56	729		144	0.0001

!

	343	128		625	4.41	1	1,024

2

Scientific Notation

Name _____

In what area of the world is it against the law to show or make films that contain kissing scenes?

To find out, find the following numbers written in scientific notation at the bottom of the page and put the corresponding letter above each.

E. 0.00000000361

E. 3,610,000,000,000,000

T. 0.0000000000361

L. 0.0000000000000361

N. 3,610,000,000,000,000,000

A. 0.00000000000000361

W. 3,610,000,000,000

G. 0.000000000361

D. 36,100,000,000

A. 0.00000000000361

I. 361,000,000,000

S. 0.00000000000000361

N. 36,100,000,000,000

B. 36,100,000,000,000,000

I. 0.00000000000000000361

3.61×10^{12} 3.61×10^{15} 3.61×10^{-15} 3.61×10^{-11}

3.61×10^{16} 3.61×10^{-9} 3.61×10^{13} 3.61×10^{-10} 3.61×10^{-12} 3.61×10^{-14} ,

3.61×10^{-18} 3.61×10^{18} 3.61×10^{10} 3.61×10^{11} 3.61×10^{-16}

Primes and Composites

Skill: prime and composite numbers

Name _____

Complete the table.

	Number	Prime or Composite	Factors
1.	56		
2.	64		
3.	97		
4.	18		
5.	45		
6.	22		
7.	59		
8.	8		
9.	41		
10.	98		
11.	70		
12.	63		
13.	17		
14.	120		
15.	61		
16.	33		
17.	78		
18.	103		
19.	84		
20.	29		

Prime Factorization

Name _____

Draw lines from the composite number to its prime factorization and then to the prime factorization written in exponential notation.

	Composite Number	Prime Factorization	Exponential Notation
1.	96	2 x 2 x 2 x 3 x 3	$2^2 \times 3^2 \times 11$
2.	52	2 x 2 x 3 x 5 x 17	$2^6 \times 5$
3.	85	3 x 3 x 3 x 7	$2^3 \times 7$
4.	315	2 x 7 x 7 x 7	$2^2 \times 13$
5.	171	2 x 2 x 2 x 2 x 2 x 3	$3^2 \times 5 \times 7$
6.	184	2 x 3 x 3 x 3 x 3	$2^4 \times 3 \times 7$
7.	945	2 x 2 x 2 x 2 x 2 x 2 x 5	5×17
8.	198	3 x 3 x 5 x 7	$3^2 \times 19$
9.	686	2 x 2 x 2 x 2 x 2 x 2 x 2 x 2	$2^3 \times 3^2$
10.	90	3 x 3 x 3 x 5 x 7	$2 \times 3^2 \times 7$
11.	126	2 x 2 x 3 x 3 x 11	$2^2 \times 3 \times 5 \times 17$
12.	72	2 x 3 x 3 x 11	$3^3 \times 7$
13.	396	2 x 2 x 2 x 23	2×7^3
14.	1,020	5 x 17	$2 \times 3^2 \times 5$
15.	256	2 x 2 x 2 x 2 x 3 x 7	$2^3 \times 23$
16.	189	2 x 2 x 2 x 7	$2^5 \times 3$
17.	162	3 x 3 x 19	2^8
18.	56	2 x 2 x 13	$2 \times 3^2 \times 11$
19.	320	2 x 3 x 3 x 7	$3^3 \times 5 \times 7$
20.	336	2 x 3 x 3 x 5	2×3^4

5

GCF

Name _____

| What was John Wayne's real name? |

Find the greatest common factor of the following pairs of numbers at the bottom of the page. Then, put the corresponding letter above each to get the answer.

A. 16, 80   O. 55, 88   A. 25, 30   S. 52, 48

I. 70, 42   I. 92, 69   O. 30, 75   R. 18, 45

H. 26, 65   N. 24, 36   M. 27, 12   C. 34, 85

I. 66, 42   N. 110, 42   L. 99, 132   R. 21, 49

O. 125, 75   E. 76, 34   R. 36, 63   M. 88, 48

M. 63, 84

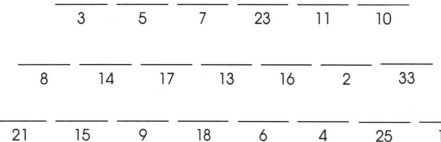

___ ___ ___ ___ ___ ___
 3   5   7   23   11   10

___ ___ ___ ___ ___ ___ ___
 8   14   17   13   16   2   33

___ ___ ___ ___ ___ ___ ___ ___
 21   15   9   18   6   4   25   12

LCM

Name _____

Draw lines from the pair of numbers in the doughnuts to their least common multiple in the coffee mugs.

14
16

198

8
21

180

22
18

108

15
10

90

18
12

200

40
25

84

26
12

35
15

112

30

16
22

36

168

54
36

102

9
30

176

20
18

156

51
34

48

16
24

6
28

105

7

Absolute Value

| Who is Quasimodo? |

Name _____

Find the integers at the bottom of the page and put the corresponding letter above each to spell out the answer to this question.

H. |18| T. |-46 + 29| H. |32 – 38| M. |-14 – 13|

E. |-12| – 17   K. |20 + -25| N. |-15| E. |2 – 16|

O. |13 + -9| A. |-12| O. 8 – |-17| C. |-20 – 2|

E. |-7| – |13| F. |-26| – 40   D. |2 + -5| C. |11| – |-42|

T. 1 – |19| H. |9| N. |17 – 33| C. |8 – 16|

R. |-5 – 19| U. |-38 + 5|

A. 1 – |-17|

| -18 | 6 | -6 | | 9 | 33 | 15 | 22 | 18 | 8 | 12 | -31 | 5 |

| 4 | -14 | | 16 | -9 | 17 | 24 | -5 | | 3 | -16 | 27 | 14 |

Order of Operations

Name _____

Put the following in increasing order.

- [ ] $(20 \div 5 \cdot 8 \div 2 \times 4) \div (25 - 16 + 11 - 7 + 3)$

- [ ] $(42 + 18 - 54) \times \sqrt{100} \div (9^2 - 11 \times 6) \times (36 - 34 + 1^4)$

- [ ] $(26 - 5^2 + \sqrt{16}) \times (70 \div 7 + 4 - 2^3) \div (4^2 - 6)$

- [ ] $8 \times 6 + 33 \div 11 - 7 \times 6 + 6^2 \div 2 - 63 \div 9 \times 2$

- [ ] $92 - (48 \div 8 \times 5 \div 3 - 2)^2 + 16 \div 4 \times 5 \div 2 \times 7 - 4 \times (20 + \sqrt{4})$

- [ ] $77 \div (7 \times 8 - 5 \times 9) \times 4 - 48 \div 2^2$

- [ ] $(20 - 9 + 28 - 17 + 7 - 24)^2 \div (99 \div 33 + \sqrt[3]{8})$

- [ ] $(4^2 - 3^2) \times (\sqrt{36} + \sqrt{144}) \div (5^2 - 2^2)$

- [ ] $(8 \times 3 - 5 \times 4 + 6^2 - 1^7 + 11 \times 2 + \sqrt[3]{8}) \div \sqrt{49}$

- [ ] $(5 \times 12 \div 10 \times 7 + 31 \times 3) \div (88 \div 11 \times 3 - 75 \div 5)$

- [ ] $(64 - 11 \times 3 + 52 \div 4 - 72 \div 8 + 3 \times 7) \div (13 - 4 + 5 - 7)$

- [ ] $84 \div (5^2 + 4 - 15) + 6 \times (\sqrt[4]{16}) + 3 \times 2 - 48 \div (11 + 15 - 23) - 72 \div (2^2 + 2^3)$

Fractions

Name _____

What are wine glasses?

To find out, reduce each of the following fractions to lowest terms and put the letter representing it above the answer at the bottom of the page.

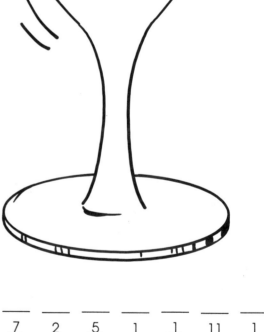

I.	$\dfrac{32}{80}$	I.	$\dfrac{35}{45}$	A.	$\dfrac{27}{33}$	
M.	$\dfrac{45}{60}$	H.	$\dfrac{36}{63}$	E.	$\dfrac{56}{64}$	
E.	$\dfrac{44}{60}$	L.	$\dfrac{30}{36}$	W.	$\dfrac{4}{44}$	
H.	$\dfrac{16}{48}$	R.	$\dfrac{6}{21}$	A.	$\dfrac{30}{54}$	
D.	$\dfrac{3}{42}$	R.	$\dfrac{28}{35}$	S.	$\dfrac{11}{66}$	
C.	$\dfrac{24}{54}$	E.	$\dfrac{35}{60}$	S.	$\dfrac{14}{26}$	
T.	$\dfrac{12}{52}$	T.	$\dfrac{21}{84}$	N.	$\dfrac{15}{100}$	
A.	$\dfrac{9}{72}$	R.	$\dfrac{36}{56}$	G.	$\dfrac{10}{36}$	
O.	$\dfrac{26}{39}$	E.	$\dfrac{12}{45}$	W.	$\dfrac{12}{64}$	
P.	$\dfrac{7}{84}$	A.	$\dfrac{24}{33}$	N.	$\dfrac{12}{40}$	

$\dfrac{3}{16}$ $\dfrac{4}{7}$ $\dfrac{5}{9}$ $\dfrac{3}{13}$ $\dfrac{3}{20}$ $\dfrac{7}{8}$ $\dfrac{8}{11}$ $\dfrac{2}{7}$ $\dfrac{7}{13}$ $\dfrac{2}{5}$ $\dfrac{5}{18}$ $\dfrac{1}{3}$ $\dfrac{1}{4}$ $\dfrac{11}{15}$ $\dfrac{1}{14}$

$\dfrac{4}{9}$ $\dfrac{2}{3}$ $\dfrac{3}{4}$ $\dfrac{1}{12}$ $\dfrac{5}{6}$ $\dfrac{1}{8}$ $\dfrac{7}{9}$ $\dfrac{3}{10}$ $\dfrac{7}{12}$ $\dfrac{9}{14}$ $\dfrac{1}{6}$ $\dfrac{1}{11}$ $\dfrac{4}{15}$ $\dfrac{9}{11}$ $\dfrac{4}{5}$

Fractions as Percents

Name _____

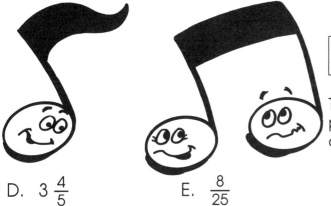

What musical group can open any safe?

To find out, write the following fractions as percents and put the letters above the answers at the bottom of the page.

D. $3\frac{4}{5}$ E. $\frac{8}{25}$ O. $\frac{9}{200}$ E. $\frac{13}{16}$

N. $\frac{11}{20}$ S. $\frac{5}{32}$ C. $2\frac{17}{40}$ N. $\frac{19}{25}$

K. $\frac{71}{80}$ T. $2\frac{1}{8}$ K. $\frac{49}{50}$ H. $2\frac{2}{10}$

O. $2\frac{1}{2}$ W. $\frac{1}{250}$ I. $\frac{73}{100}$ L. $3\frac{3}{4}$

| 76% | 81.25% | 0.4% | | 88.75% | 73% | 380% | 15.625% |

| | 250% | 55% | | 212.5% | 220% | 32% |

| | 375% | 4.5% | 242.5% | 98% |

11

Decimals as Percents

Name _____

Circle the letters representing decimals that have been correctly written as percents.
Read these from top to bottom to finish the following sentence:

There is an odd law in New Jersey concerning food. This law makes it illegal to:

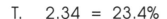

T.	2.34	= 23.4%
S.	4.8	= 480%
A.	0.0005	= 0.5%
M.	0.63	= 6.3%
L.	0.0006	= 0.06%
R.	0.47	= 4.7%
O.	3.04	= 30.04%
U.	0.0495	= 4.95%
N.	2.994	= 29.94%
R.	6.0	= 600%
D.	8.088	= 80.88%
P.	0.875	= 87.5%
C.	0.62	= 620%
K.	0.05	= 50%

B.	0.073	= 73%
A.	0.153	= 153%
S.	3.4	= 340%
T.	20.1	= 201%
H.	1.39	= 13.9%
O.	0.099	= 9.9%
R.	0.0004	= 0.4%
U.	1.111	= 111.1%
S.	6.006	= 600.06%
E.	0.0112	= 11.2%
P.	0.0025	= 0.25%
I.	7.4	= 74%
C.	0.8256	= 8.256%
Y.	9.09	= 90.9%

Fractions, Decimals and Percents

Name _____

Complete the table.

	Fraction	Decimal	Percent
1.	$\frac{7}{8}$		
2.			95%
3.		0.008	
4.			1.2%
5.	$\frac{19}{40}$		
6.		6.66	
7.		0.455	
8.			38%
9.	$\frac{17}{25}$		
10.			2.1%
11.		0.1875	
12.	$5\frac{4}{5}$		
13.			45%
14.			3.125%
15.		0.99	
16.	$8\frac{3}{100}$		

Rational and Irrational Numbers

Name _____

What do you give a piglet with diaper rash?

Circle the letters representing irrational numbers. Read these from the top down to get the answer.

A. 0.063490634906...

D. 618.49875234920006

O. 55.06620662066200662...

R. 0.0000000500050005...

F. 0.213699213699213...

I. 98.68788898182838485818...

L. 14.68911391139113...

T. 0.004872368777712

N. 0.00000000000000987...

A. 8.23538297642898989...

N. 0.438666666666666464646...

R. 23.0000675526755267...

K. 4.23887238872388877238...

T. 0.0091130412568444424242...

M. 6.44444455555686876856...

O. 38.410234556823782828...

I. 555.5555555555555685685...

E. 9.99854443222227884...

L. 0.643896264389626643896...

R. 29.458895113203203203...

N. 1.73085249765100325987...

S. 0.00000071012684467676...

T. 8.0123688924589245892...

M. 1,000.048723114876893434343...

B. 97.04568773456877345...

C. 1.835001687306333333...

T. 0.004384384381438438243...

E. 0.04896888139688813968...

S. 9.2213344522133445221...

R. 0.000000000000000068456845...

D. 382.500563400300200200200...

14

Mixed Practice

Name _____

1. Write as a percent.

   1.005

2. Is this number rational or irrational?

   0.034134413444134...

3. Write the numeral.

   8^3

4. List all the factors of 90.

5. Write in scientific notation.

   89,600,000,000,000,000

6. Find the LCM of the pair of numbers.

   25, 6

7. Solve.

   $(3^2 + 11) - 4 + 25 \div 5 \times \sqrt[3]{8}$

8. Solve.

   $-8 + |-20|$

9. Write in standard form.

   1.41×10^{-13}

10. Find the GCF of the pair of numbers.

    35, 56

11. Write in lowest terms.

    $\dfrac{40}{96}$

12. Write as a percent.

    $\dfrac{15}{16}$

13. Solve.

    $(0.5)^8 \div (0.5)^5$

14. Write as a decimal and as a fraction.

    32.5%

15. Write in lowest terms.

    $\dfrac{72}{99}$

16. Write the prime factorization of 1,980.

Metric Units of Length

Name _____

Complete the table.

	kilometer km	hectometer hm	dekameter dam	meter m	decimeter dm	centimeter cm	millimeter mm
1.				8			
2.					320		
3.			6.7				
4.		0.95					
5.							730
6.	0.001						
7.					46		
8.			2				
9.						88	
10.		31					
11.				15			
12.							9
13.					0.05		
14.	7						
15.				0.43			
16.						6	

Metric Units of Capacity

Name _____

Fill in the missing units.

1. 81 daL = 8,100 _____

2. 20 cL = 0.02 _____

3. 3.6 L = 0.0036 _____

4. 225 dL = 22,500 _____

5. 0.05 kL = 5,000 _____

6. 18 hL = 1.8 _____

7. 28 mL = 0.028 _____

8. 31,000 mL = 0.031 _____

9. 0.4 cL = 4 _____

10. 40 L = 400 _____

11. 731 dL = 7.31 _____

12. 5 daL = 0.5 _____

13. 0.009 hL = 9 _____

14. 62 L = 6,200 _____

15. 1 kL = 100,000 _____

16. 1.5 cL = 15 _____

Fill in the missing numbers.

17. 7.6 daL = _____ cL

18. 380 hL = _____ mL

19. 444 mL = _____ hL

20. 0.007 dL = _____ cL

21. 0.8 dL = _____ daL

22. 6.5 mL = _____ dL

23. 27 kL = _____ L

24. 1.15 L = _____ mL

25. 0.003 L = _____ hL

26. 28 cL = _____ hL

27. 0.98 hL = _____ cL

28. 4.02 dL = _____ mL

29. 11 cL = _____ kL

30. 0.36 kL = _____ cL

31. 2.95 kL = _____ daL

32. 700 daL = _____ kL

Metric Units of Weight

Skill: metric units of weight

Name ____________________

Complete the table.

	kilogram kg	hectogram hg	dekagram dag	gram g	decigram dg	centigram cg	milligram mg
1.	0.005						
2.				3			
3.					85		
4.		2.5					
5.							602
6.			8.9				
7.		28.1					
8.						1.2	
9.				4.6			
10.		7					
11.			3				
12.							71.5
13.					0.06		
14.				43.01			
15.	39						
16.						512	

Temperature

Name _____

What do you call a duck with fangs?

Find the Celsius temperatures for the following Kelvin temperatures at the bottom of the page and put the corresponding letter above each to solve the riddle.

C. 287.15 K   U. 374.15 K

K. 257.15 K   T. 293.35 K

L. 328.65 K   U. 207 K   O. 269.15 K   A. 228.4 K

A. 393.15 K   C. 302 K   U. 285.15 K

                      N. 306.9 K   Q. 167.5 K

_____ _____ _____ _____ _____
28.85° C   -4° C   101° C   33.75° C   20.2° C

_____ _____ _____ _____ _____ _____ _____ _____
-105.65° C -66.15° C 120° C   14° C   -16° C   12° C   55.5° C -44.75° C

Elapsed Time

Name _____

1.
Lethargic Larry left his loft at 1:30 p.m. and arrived at Peppy Pete's place at 6:00 p.m. How long did it take Larry to get there?

2.
Worldly Wanda is flying from San Diego to Las Vegas. She will depart at 6:35 a.m. Pacific time and will arrive at 8:10 a.m. Pacific time. How long is the flight?

3.
Athletic Agnes left her abode at 2:10 p.m. and jogged to Lazy Lucy's lake house. She arrived at 4:55 p.m. How long did it take Agnes?

4.
Bewildered Barry took the bus from Columbia, MO, to Peoria, IL. He departed at 12:11 a.m. Central time and arrived at 6:02 a.m. Central time. How long was the trip?

5.
Convict Carl took the ferry from San Francisco to Alcatraz. The ferry departed at 3:33 p.m. and arrived at 4:17 p.m. How long was the ferry ride?

6.
Tacky Tom took the train from Stamford, CT, to Manhattan. He departed at 9:53 a.m. and arrived at 10:38 a.m. How long was the ride?

7.
Sunseeking Sarah is flying from Newark, NJ, to Orlando, FL. She will depart at 10:06 a.m. Eastern time and will arrive at 1:32 p.m. Eastern time. How long is the flight?

8.
Cycling Cyrus rode his bike from Boulder to Colorado Springs. He departed at 11:45 a.m. and arrived at 7:20 p.m. How long did the journey take?

9.
Nell the New Yorker took the subway from Queens to downtown Manhattan. She departed at 5:12 p.m. and arrived at 6:08 p.m. How long was the subway ride?

10.
Touring Tammy drove from San Diego to San Francisco. She left at 5:40 a.m. Pacific time and arrived at 7:22 p.m. Pacific time. How long was the trip?

11.
Randy the rancher flew from Phoenix, AZ, to Butte, MT. He departed at 11:59 a.m. Mountain time and arrived at 4:06 p.m. Mountain time. How long was the flight?

12.
Patti the politician took the train from Washington, D.C., to Grand Central Terminal in New York City. She departed at 8:32 a.m. Eastern time and arrived at 10:15 a.m. Eastern time. How long was the train ride?

Mixed Practice

1. Write the missing unit.

   73.6 hm = 73,600 _____

2. Give the following in degrees Celsius:

   373.05 K

3. Write the missing number.

   515 L = _____ kL

4. Molly the mountain biker departed at 7:55 a.m. and arrived at her destination at 9:10 a.m. How long did the journey take?

5. Write the missing unit and number.

   58 mL = 0.058 _____ = _____ cL

6. Give the Kelvin temperature.

   -45°C

7. Write the missing unit and number.

   0.004 kg = _____ cg = 4 _____

8. Flying Freda flew from San Antonio, TX, to Duluth, MN. She departed at 11:25 a.m. Central time and arrived at 4:53 p.m. Central time. How long was her flight?

9. Write the missing number.

   2.5 dg = _____ hg

10. Give the Kelvin temperature.

    30.85° C

11. Write the missing number.

    0.0007 mm = _____ dm

12. Sightseeing Sara took a bus from Charlotte, NC, to Boston, MA. She departed at 2:37 p.m. Eastern time and arrived at 4:20 p.m. Eastern time the following day. How long was the bus ride?

13. Write the missing number.

    361.9 mg = _____ dag

14. Write the missing unit.

    0.26 dL = 0.00026 _____

Units of Length

Fill in the missing numbers.

Name _____

1. 4 ft 9 in. = _____ in.

2. 3 mi = _____ yd

3. 8 yd 1 ft = _____ in.

4. 4 yd 21 in. = _____ in.

5. 6 yd 2 ft = _____ in.

6. 7 yd 2 ft = _____ ft

7. 96 in. = _____ ft

8. 12,320 yd = _____ mi

9. 324 in. = _____ yd

10. 54 ft = _____ yd

11. 8 ft 11 in. = _____ in.

12. 5 mi = _____ ft

13. 180 in. = _____ yd

14. 4 yd 1 ft = _____ ft

15. $4 \frac{1}{3}$ yd = _____ ft

Fill in the missing numbers.

16.
```
   8 yd  2 ft
 - 6 yd  1 ft
_____
```

17.
```
  10 ft  7 in.
 + 5 ft  7 in.
_____
```

18.
```
  11 yd
 - 6 yd  5 in.
_____
```

19.
```
   4 yd  19 in.
 + 1 yd  17 in.
_____
```

20.
```
   5 ft   2 in.
 - 3 ft  10 in.
_____
```

21.
```
   7 ft  5 in.
 + 3 ft  9 in.
_____
```

22.
```
   6 yd  2 ft
 + 3 yd  2 ft
_____
```

23.
```
   2 yd  1 in.
 -      11 in.
_____
```

24.
```
  12 yd  1 ft
 - 10 yd  2 ft
_____
```

---

25. How many inches are there in 2 yd 9 in.?

26. How many yards are there in 36 ft?

27. How many yards are there in 5 mi?

28. How many feet are there in 19 yd?

29. How many inches are there in $7 \frac{1}{2}$ yd?

30. How many miles are there in 21,120 ft?

Units of Area

Name _____

What do you say to a high fashion baby?

To find out, find the missing numbers at the bottom of the page and put the corresponding letter above each.

C. 7,040 a = _____ mi²

G. 5 yd² = _____ ft²

I. 3,888 in.² = _____ yd²   O. 3 ft² = _____ in.²

C. 234 ft² = _____ yd²   U. 7 mi² = _____ a   C. 108 ft² = _____ yd²

I. 217,800 ft² = _____ a   G. 2 yd² = _____ in.²   G. 864 in.² = _____ ft²

U. 3 a = _____ ft²   C. 16,848 in.² = _____ yd   O. 11 ft² = _____ in.²

___ ___ ___ ___ ___   ___ ___ ___ ___ ___
6   4,480   11   13   3   2,592 130,680 26   12   5

___ ___ ___
45   432   1,584

Units of Volume

What is Shamu's favorite game show?

Name _____

To find out, find the missing numbers at the bottom of the page and put the corresponding letter above each.

N. 243 ft³ = _____ yd³   A. 14 yd³ = _____ ft³

A. 6 ft³ = _____ in.³   H. 139,968 in.³ = _____ yd³

E. 12,096 in.³ = _____ ft³   U. 216 ft³ = _____ yd³

T. 3 ½ ft³ = _____ in.³   N. 6,912 in.³ = _____ ft³

A. 9 yd³ = _____ ft³   T. 2 yd³ = _____ in.³

M. 7,776 in.³ = _____ ft³   T. 5 ft³ = _____ in.³

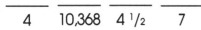

4	10,368	4 ½	7

93,312	3	378	6,048

8,640	8	9	243

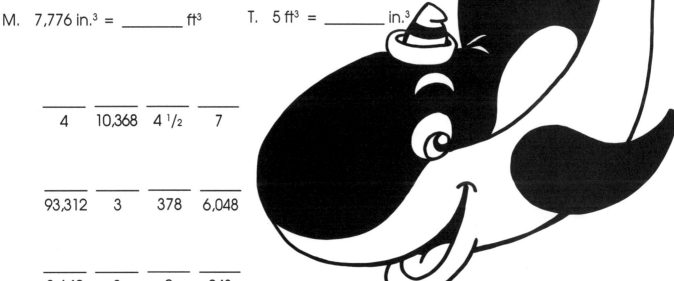

24

Units of Liquid Measure

Name _____

What do you say to your nagging music teacher?

To find out, find the missing numbers at the bottom of the page and put the corresponding letter above each.

F. 5c = _____ fl oz   C. 7 gal = _____ pt

Y. 34 qt = _____ gal   E. 9 qt = _____ pt

B. 11 c = _____ pt   T. 6 pt = _____ c

O. 11 qt = _____ c   A. 28 fl oz = _____ c

G. 15 pt = _____ qt   M. 5 pt = _____ fl oz

F. 48 fl oz = _____ qt   H. 13 gal = _____ qt

___ ___ ___   ___ ___ ___
7 ½ 18 12   44 1 ½ 40

___ ___   ___ ___ ___ ___ !
80 8 ½   5 ½ 3 ½ 56 52

Units of Weight

Skill: units of weight

Name _____

In Waterloo, NE, barbers are banned from doing something between 7 a.m. and 7 p.m. What can't they do?

Circle the incorrect inequalities and read these from top to bottom to get the answer about this unusual law.

T. 88 oz = 5 $\frac{1}{2}$ lb

E. 2 $\frac{1}{2}$ T = 4,500 lb

L. 8 lb = 128 oz

L. 6,000 lb = 3 T

I. 7 $\frac{1}{4}$ lb = 116 oz

A. 2 $\frac{1}{4}$ lb = 44 oz

N. $\frac{3}{4}$ T = 1,500 lb

T. 145 oz = 9 lb

G. 112 oz = 7 lb

E. 8 $\frac{3}{4}$ lb = 140 oz

R. 8,000 lb = 4 T

C. 68 oz = 4 $\frac{1}{4}$ lb

O. 17 $\frac{1}{2}$ lb = 284 oz

E. 5 T = 10,000 lb

L. 10 lb = 160 oz

N. 975 lb = 4 $\frac{3}{4}$ T

E. 64 oz = 4 lb

R. 1 $\frac{1}{2}$ lb = 24 oz

I. 300 oz = 19 lb

Y. 3 $\frac{3}{4}$ T = 7,500 lb

O. 9 $\frac{1}{2}$ T = 18,500 lb

G. 12,000 lb = 6 T

U. 320 oz = 20 lb

N. 7 lb = 120 oz

R. 15 $\frac{1}{4}$ lb = 244 oz

S. 12 T = 22,000 lb

T. 188 oz = 11 $\frac{3}{4}$ lb

26

©Instructional Fair, Inc.

Mixed Practice

Name _____

1. How many acres is 6 square miles?

2. The soda can held 12 fl oz. How many cups is this?

3. How many inches are there in 6 yd 1 ft 8 in.?

4. Solve.

$$\begin{array}{r} 4 \text{ lb } \ \ 7 \text{ oz} \\ + \ 6 \text{ lb } 11 \text{ oz} \\ \hline \end{array}$$

5. Fill in the missing number.

$$4 \, {}^1/_4 \text{ ft}^2 = \text{_____} \text{ in.}^2$$

6. Fill in the missing number.

$$5 \text{ qt} = \text{_____} \text{ fl oz}$$

7. Fill in the missing number.

$$9 \, {}^1/_2 \text{ ft}^3 = \text{_____} \text{ in.}^3$$

8. Fill in the missing number.

$$11 \text{ ft } 8 \text{ in.} = \text{_____} \text{ in.}$$

9. How many cubic feet are there in 12 cubic yards?

10. How many cups are in 7 gallons?

11. Fill in the missing number.

$$186{,}624 \text{ in.}^3 = \text{_____} \text{ yd}^3$$

12. Solve.

$$\begin{array}{r} 10 \text{ ft } \ 4 \text{ in.} \\ - \ 7 \text{ ft } \ 9 \text{ in.} \\ \hline \end{array}$$

13. How many ounces are in one ton?

14. How many square feet are in an acre?

Angle Measure

Name _____

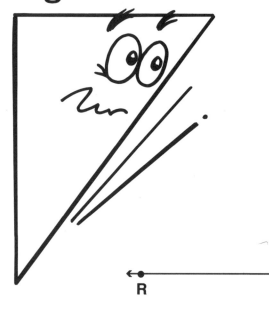

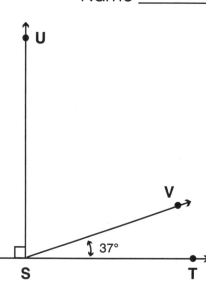

Name:

1. two acute angles _____

2. a straight angle _____

3. an obtuse angle _____

4. two right angles _____

5. a pair of complementary angles _____

6. two pairs of supplementary angles _____

7. the measure of ∠UST _____

8. the measure of ∠RSV _____

9. the measure of ∠USV _____

State each of the following angles' complement.

10. m∠K = 12°   11. m∠A = 73°   12. m∠X = 54°

13. m∠N = 85°   14. m∠D = 29°   15. m∠T = 46°

State if the following angles are acute, right or obtuse and give the measure of a supplement to each angle.

16. m∠B = 135°   17. m∠S = 114°   18. m∠C = 88°

19. m∠R = 33°   20. m∠W = 90°   21. m∠E = 162°

28

Lines

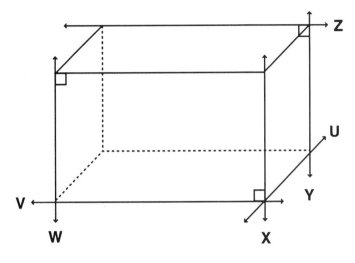

1. Which lines are ll to line X? _____

2. Which lines are ⊥ to line V? _____

3. Which lines are ⊥ to line Y? _____

4. Name at least three sets of skew lines. _____

5. Name two transversals. _____

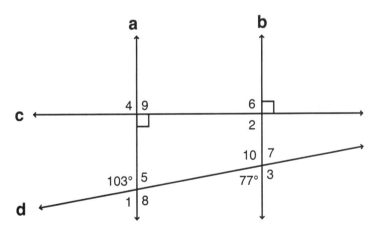

a ll b
a ⊥ c
b ⊥ c

6. Name two transversals of lines a and b. _____

7. Name two transversals of lines c and d. _____

8. What is the measure of ∠3? _____

9. What is the measure of ∠8? _____

10. What is the measure of ∠10? _____

11. What is the measure of ∠7? _____

12. Which other angles have the same measure as ∠7? _____

13. Name the right angles. _____

Triangles

Name _____

Name each triangle according to the information given.

1.
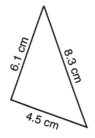

2.
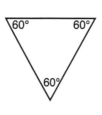

3.

4.

5.

6.

7.

8.
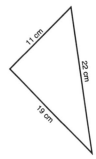

9.
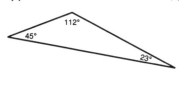

10.
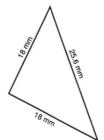

11.

12.
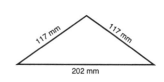

13.

14.

15.
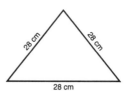

16.
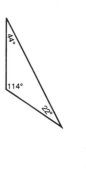

17.
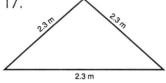

18.

19.
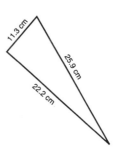

20.

Triangles

Name _____

| Why did Bart Simpson get suspended from the softball team? |

Find the measure of the third angle for each of the triangles at the bottom of the page. Put the corresponding letter above each correct measure to get the punchline.

H.
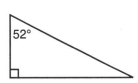
52°

M.
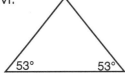
53° 53°

O.
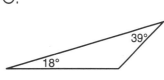
39°
18°

I.

99° 54°

O.
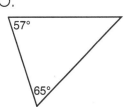
57°
65°

G.

18°
121°

R.
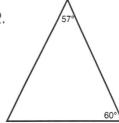
57°
60°

A.
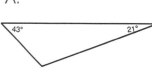
43° 21°

R.

25°
22°

I.
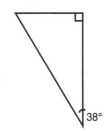
38°

E.
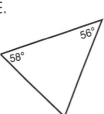
56°
58°

T.
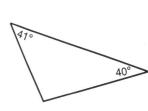
41°
40°

F.
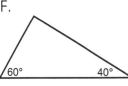
60° 40°

N.
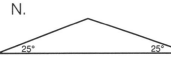
25° 25°

H.
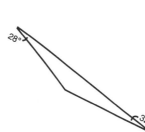
28°
32°

T.
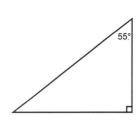
55°

| 80° | 123° | 133° | | 38° | 52° | 99° | 35° | 27° | 130° | 41° |

| | 116° | | 120° | 58° | 74° | 66° | 63° |

31

Polygons

Name _____

Name each polygon and find the sum of the measures of the angles.

1.

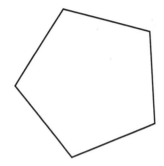

2.

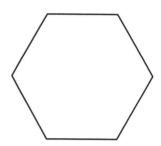

3.

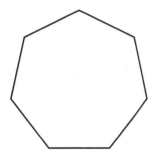

4.

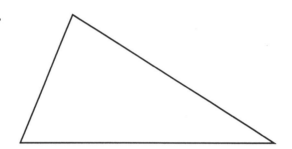

5.

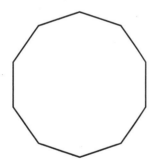

6.

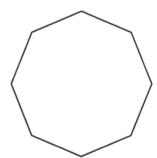

7.

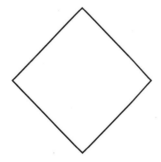

8.

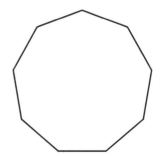

32

Polygons

Name _____

In Omaha, NE, parents can be arrested if their children do what?

To find out, find the degree measure of C in each polygon. Then, find this answer at the bottom of the page and put the corresponding letter above each answer.

H.
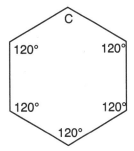

N.
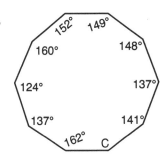

H.
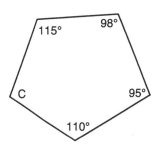

R.
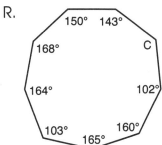

U.
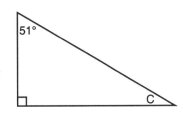

B.
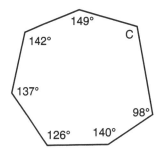

R.
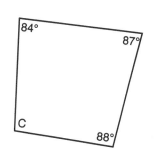

U.
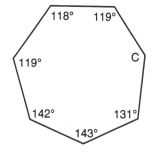

C.
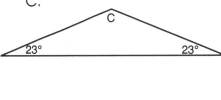

I.
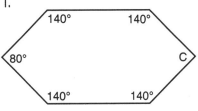

C.
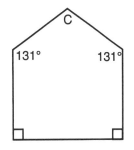

P.
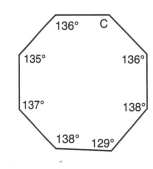

108°	128°	105°	131°		80°	130°		98°	120°	39°	101°	134°	122°

Circles

Name _____

Name the following parts of the circle below.

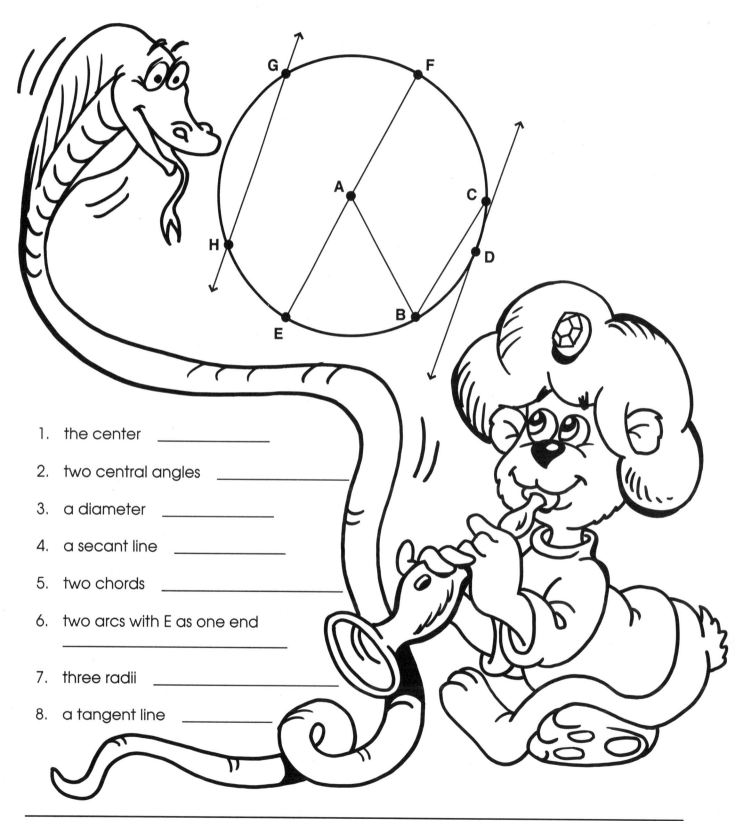

1. the center _____

2. two central angles _____

3. a diameter _____

4. a secant line _____

5. two chords _____

6. two arcs with E as one end
   _____

7. three radii _____

8. a tangent line _____

Construction—Line Segments and Angles

Name _____

Using a compass and a straight edge, construct a segment congruent to:

1.

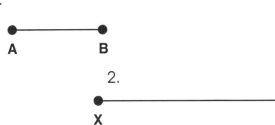

A   B

3.

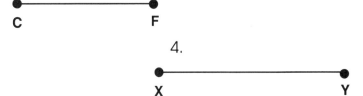

C   F

2.

X   Y

4.

X   Y

Construct an angle congruent to:

5.

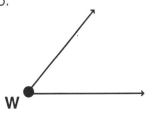

W

6.

D

7.

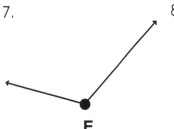

E

8.

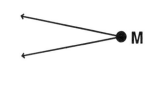

M

Construct the perpendicular bisector of:

9.

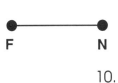

F   N

11.

Q   R

10.

O   P

12.

B   T

Bisect the angles:

13.

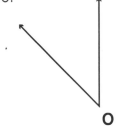

O

14.

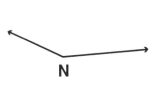

N

15.

P

16.

G

Construction—
Congruent Triangles

Name _____

Using a compass and a straight edge, use SSS congruence to construct triangles congruent to the following:

1.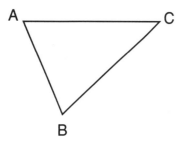

2.

3.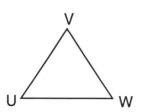

4.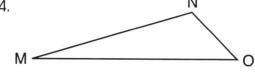

5.

6.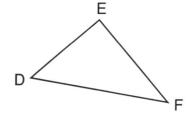

7.

8.

9.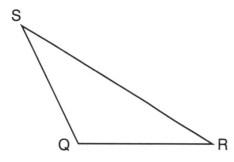

10.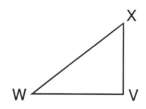

Construction— Congruent Triangles

Name _____

Using a compass and a straight edge, use SAS congruence to construct triangles congruent to the following:

1.

2.

3.
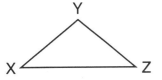

4.

5.
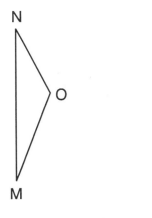

6.
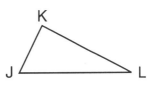

7.

8.
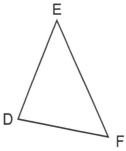

9.
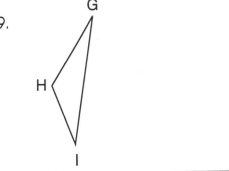

10.
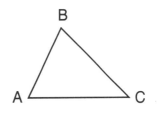

Construction—
Congruent Triangles

Name _____

Using a compass and a straight edge, use ASA congruence to construct triangles congruent to the following:

1.
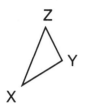

2.
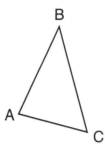

3.

4.
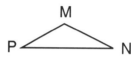

5.
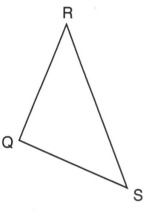

6.
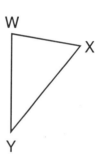

7.

8.
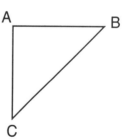

9.
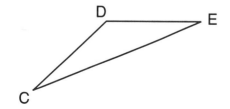

10.
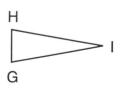

Congruent Triangles

Name _____

State if the triangles have SSS, SAS or ASA congruence.

1.
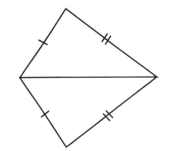

2.
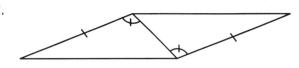

3.
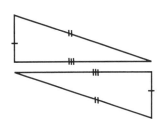

4.
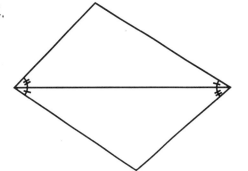

5.
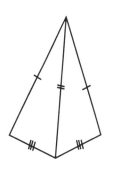

6.
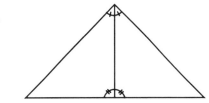

7.
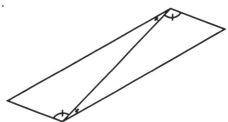

8.
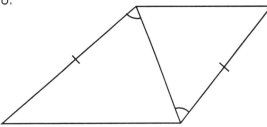

9.
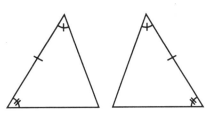

10.
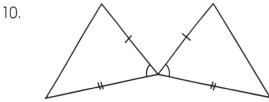

Similar Triangles

Name _____

| What do you call a crazy pickle? |

To find out, find the length x for each pair of similar triangles. Then, find this answer at the bottom of the page and put the corresponding letter above the answer.

A.
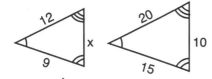

F.

I.
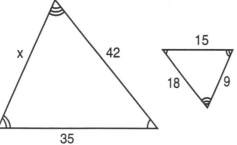

A.
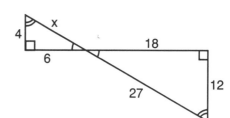

L.
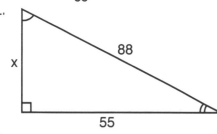

D.
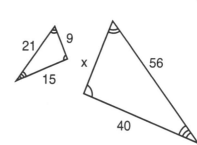

Y.
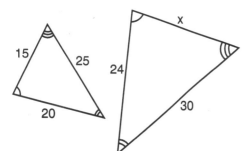

L.
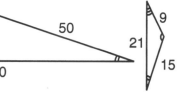

F.
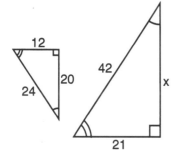

D.
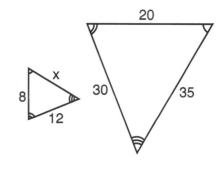

___ ___ ___ ___ ___ ___ ___ ___ ___ ___
9   24   6   35   36   18   14   21   30   33

Tangent Ratios

Name _____

It is illegal to hold what in Key West, Florida?

To find out the answer to this riddle, locate tan X at the bottom of the page and put the corresponding letter above each tangent ratio.

A.
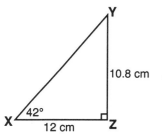

R.
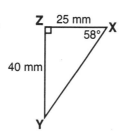

S.
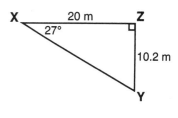

T.
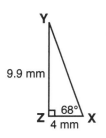

C.
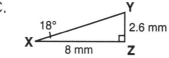

E.
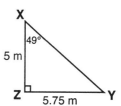

U.
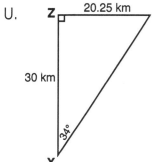

R.
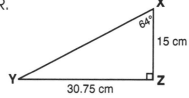

T.
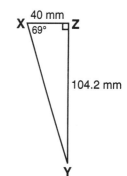

L.
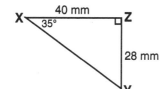

E.
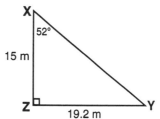

____ ____ ____ ____ ____ ____   ____ ____ ____ ____ ____
2.605 0.675 1.6 2.475 0.7 1.15   2.05 0.9 0.325 1.28 0.51

Table of Tangent Ratios

Name _____

Tangent ratios are rounded to the nearest thousandth.

Angle	Tangent	Angle	Tangent	Angle	Tangent	Angle	Tangent	Angle	Tangent
0°	0.000	20°	0.364	40°	0.839	60°	1.732	80°	5.671
1°	0.018	21°	0.384	41°	0.869	61°	1.804	81°	6.314
2°	0.035	22°	0.404	42°	0.900	62°	1.881	82°	7.115
3°	0.052	23°	0.425	43°	0.933	63°	1.963	83°	8.144
4°	0.070	24°	0.445	44°	0.966	64°	2.050	84°	9.514
5°	0.088	25°	0.466	45°	1.000	65°	2.145	85°	11.430
6°	0.105	26°	0.488	46°	1.036	66°	2.246	86°	14.301
7°	0.123	27°	0.510	47°	1.072	67°	2.356	87°	19.081
8°	0.141	28°	0.532	48°	1.111	68°	2.475	88°	28.636
9°	0.158	29°	0.554	49°	1.150	69°	2.605	89°	57.290
10°	0.176	30°	0.577	50°	1.192	70°	2.748		
11°	0.194	31°	0.601	51°	1.235	71°	2.904		
12°	0.213	32°	0.625	52°	1.280	72°	3.078		
13°	0.231	33°	0.649	53°	1.327	73°	3.271		
14°	0.249	34°	0.675	54°	1.376	74°	3.487		
15°	0.268	35°	0.700	55°	1.428	75°	3.732		
16°	0.287	36°	0.727	56°	1.483	76°	4.011		
17°	0.306	37°	0.754	57°	1.540	77°	4.332		
18°	0.325	38°	0.781	58°	1.600	78°	4.705		
19°	0.344	39°	0.810	59°	1.664	79°	5.145		

Find the degree measure for ∠X.

1. tan X ≈ 0.727

2. tan X ≈ 11.430

3. tan X ≈ 0.364

4. tan X ≈ 0.810

5. tan X ≈ 0.194

6. tan X ≈ 0.510

7. tan X ≈ 1.280

8. tan X ≈ 0.425

9. tan X ≈ 1.235

10. tan X ≈ 19.081

11. tan X ≈ 0.158

12. tan X ≈ 4.332

Find each tangent ratio.

13. tan 70°

14. tan 26°

15. tan 3°

16. tan 82°

17. tan 78°

18. tan 16°

19. tan 49°

20. tan 22°

21. tan 31°

22. tan 53°

23. tan 19°

24. tan 64°

Mixed Practice

1. Find the length x for the pair of similar triangles.

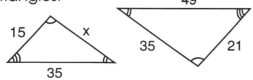

2. Find the degree measure of x.

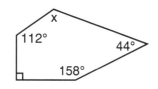

3. What part of the circle is line AB?

   What is $\overline{AB}$?

   What is $\overline{XY}$?

   What is $\overset{\frown}{ZB}$?

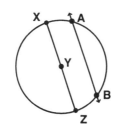

4. Write if the angle is acute, straight, right or obtuse. What is its supplementary angle?

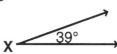

5. Give the tangent of ∠X to the nearest thousandth.

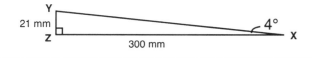

6. Bisect the angle.

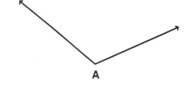

7. What type of congruence do the triangles have?

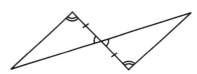

8. Name the type of triangle according to the length of its sides.

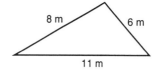

9. Construct a triangle congruent to △ABC using SSS, SAS or ASA congruence.

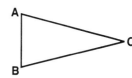

10. Name the type of triangle according to the measure of its angles.

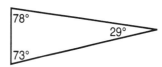

11. Name the polygon.

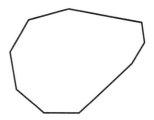

12. Find the measure of the third angle.

Perimeter

Name _____

Find the sum of the perimeters that make up Paulie the polygon baby.

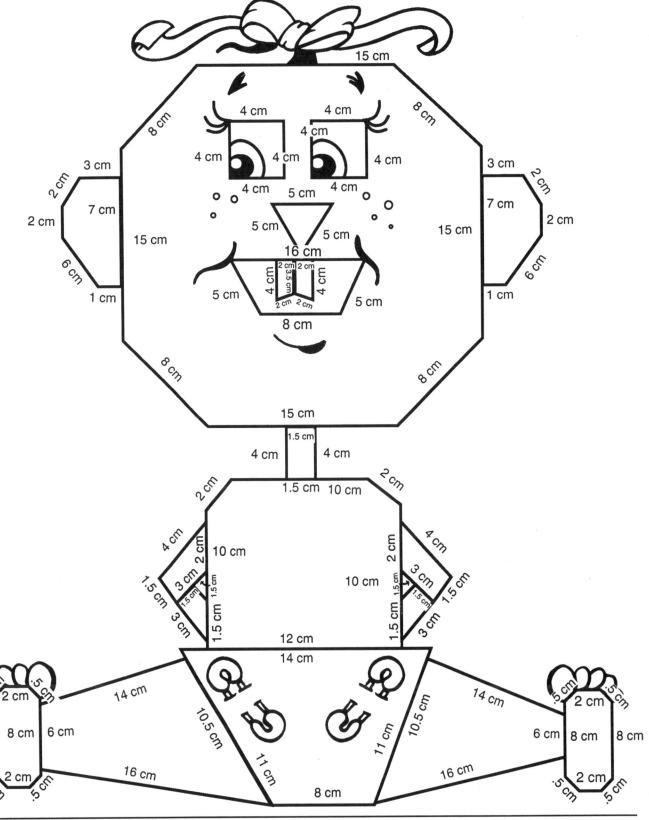

Area

Name _____

| What are as unique as fingerprints? |

To find out, find the areas of the following shapes. Then, find the answers at the bottom of the page and put the corresponding letter above each answer.

S.
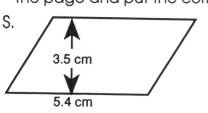
3.5 cm
5.4 cm

I.

8.3 cm

N.
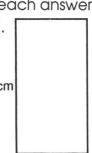
9 cm
2.6 cm

U.
8.5 cm
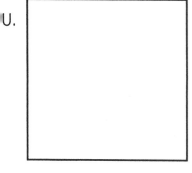

R.
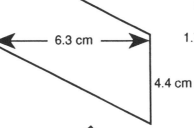
6.3 cm
4.4 cm

O.
1.7 cm
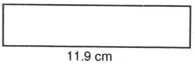
11.9 cm

N.
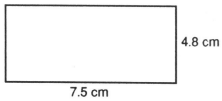
4.8 cm
7.5 cm

T.
5.1 cm
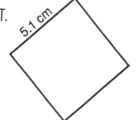

P.
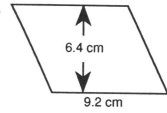
6.4 cm
9.2 cm

E.
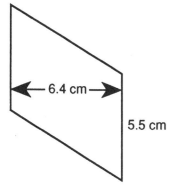
6.4 cm
5.5 cm

T.
7.2 cm
4.5 cm
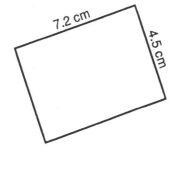

G.
2.3 cm

_____ _____ _____ _____ _____ _____
32.4 cm²   20.23 cm²   36 cm²   5.29 cm²   72.25 cm²   35.2 cm²

_____ _____ _____ _____ _____ _____
58.88 cm²   27.72 cm²   68.89 cm²   23.4 cm²   26.01 cm²   18.9 cm²

Area

Name _____

Find the area of each figure.

1.

5.8 cm

2.
6 m
10.5 m

3.
18 cm
19.8 cm
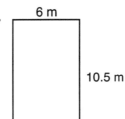

4.
8 in.
1 in.
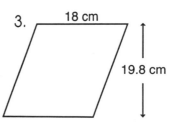

5.
4.9 m
2.7 m
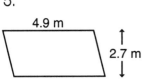

6.
22.2 cm
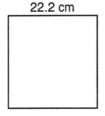

7.
3.8 m
11.6 m
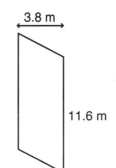

8.
14.2 cm
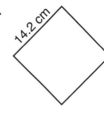

9.
18 ft
13 ft
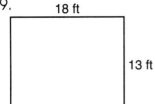

10.
2 in.

11.
16 cm
3.28 cm
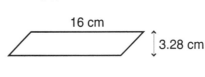

12.
64 cm
23 cm
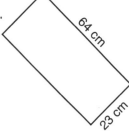

13.
23 ft
17 ft
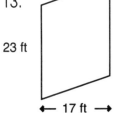

14.
11.7 m
8.8 m
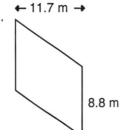

15.
29 ft
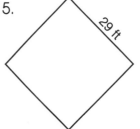

16.
38.5 cm
42.8 cm
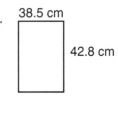

17. Square:
s = 4.2 cm

18. Parallelogram:
b = 2 ft, h = 3 ft

19. Rectangle:
l = 8.5 m, w = 6 m

20. Parallelogram:
b = 11 in.
h = 18 in.

21. Rectangle:
l = 6.4 cm
w = 8 cm

22. Square:
s = 53 m

23. Parallelogram:
b = 23 cm
h = 52 cm

24. Rectangle:
l = 4 m, w = 2.7 m

Area

Name

Thousands of years after his time, Mr. Geometric Caveman left these cave drawings for you to decode. Find the area of each of the triangles and trapezoids. Then, use the cave drawing decoder box to decipher his message.

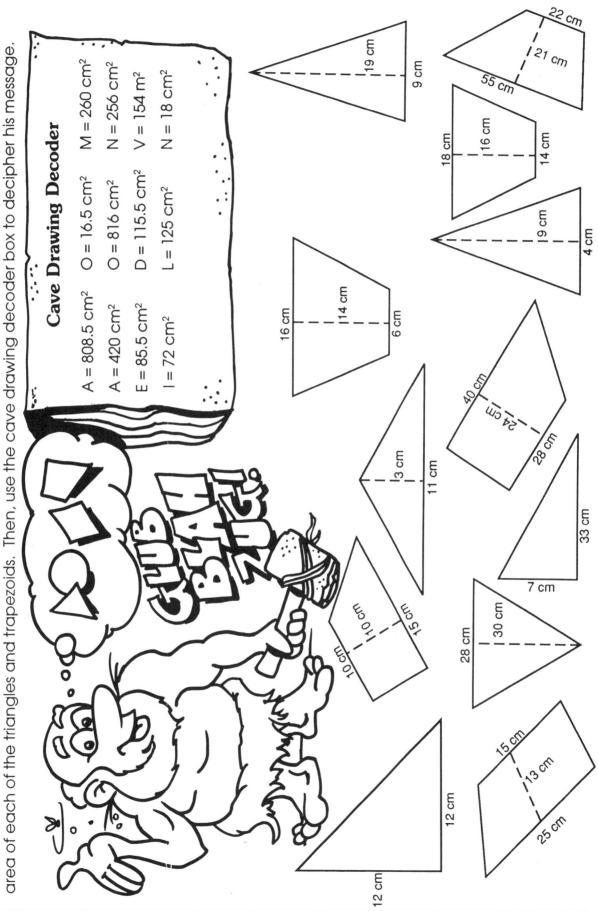

Cave Drawing Decoder

A = 808.5 cm²   O = 16.5 cm²   M = 260 cm²

A = 420 cm²   O = 816 cm²   N = 256 cm²

E = 85.5 cm²   D = 115.5 cm²   V = 154 m²

I = 72 cm²   L = 125 cm²   N = 18 cm²

Area

Name _____

Find the area of each figure.

1.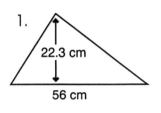
22.3 cm
56 cm

2.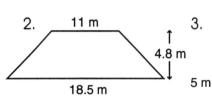
11 m
4.8 m
18.5 m

3.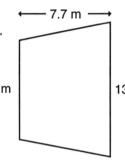
7.7 m
5 m
13 m

4.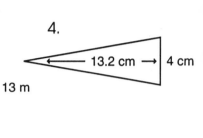
13.2 cm
4 cm

5.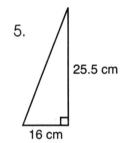
25.5 cm
16 cm

6.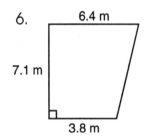
6.4 m
7.1 m
3.8 m

7.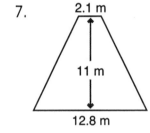
2.1 m
11 m
12.8 m

8.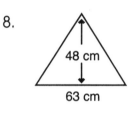
48 cm
63 cm

9.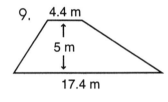
4.4 m
5 m
17.4 m

10.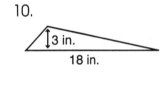
3 in.
18 in.

11.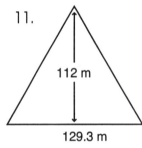
112 m
129.3 m

12.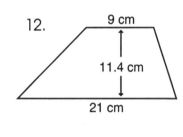
9 cm
11.4 cm
21 cm

13.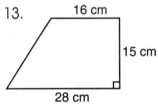
16 cm
15 cm
28 cm

14.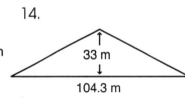
33 m
104.3 m

15.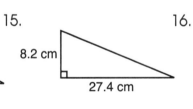
8.2 cm
27.4 cm

16.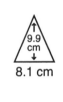
9.9 cm
8.1 cm

17. Triangle:
    b = 24 cm
    h = 17.7 cm

18. Trapezoid:
    b_1 = 4.3 m
    b_2 = 11 m
    h = 14.9 m

19. Trapezoid:
    b_1 = 118 ft
    b_2 = 126 ft
    h = 122 ft

20. Triangle:
    b = 5 cm
    h = 46.5 cm

21. Trapezoid:
    b_1 = 0.8 m
    b_2 = 0.5 m
    h = 0.6 m

22. Triangle:
    b = 132 in.
    h = 56 in.

23. Triangle:
    b = 14.8 m
    h = 19.7 m

24. Trapezoid:
    b_1 = 10.2 cm
    b_2 = 9.6 cm
    h = 8.2 cm

Circumference

Name _____

| Why do nuns watch soap operas? |

To find out, find the circumference for each circle at the bottom of the page and put the corresponding letter above each. Use 3.14 for π.

I.
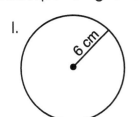
6 cm

E.
21 cm

Y.
3.8 cm

T.
16.5 cm

H.
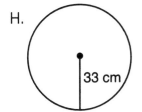
33 cm

A.
11.2 cm

N.
15.5 cm

H.
9.4 cm

T.
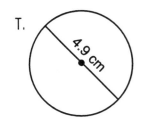
4.9 cm

E.
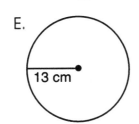
13 cm

T.
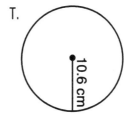
10.6 cm

E.
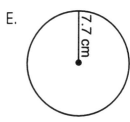
7.7 cm

T.
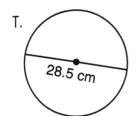
28.5 cm

O.
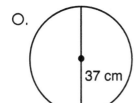
37 cm

B.
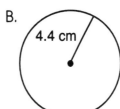
4.4 cm

T.
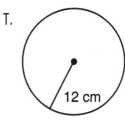
12 cm

I.
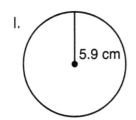
5.9 cm

G.
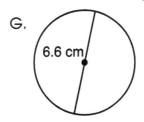
6.6 cm

H.
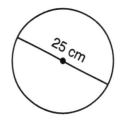
25 cm

| 75.36 cm | 29.516 cm | 52.36 cm | 23.864 cm | | 20.724 cm | 65.94 cm | 15.386 cm | | 37.052 cm | 48.67 cm | 51.81 cm | 116.18 cm |

| | 89.49 cm | 207.24 cm | 81.64 cm | | 78.5 cm | 70.336 cm | 27.632 cm | 37.68 cm | 66.568 cm |

!

Circumference

Name _____

Find the sum of the circumferences of the circles that make up Penelope Piglet.
Use 3.14 for π.

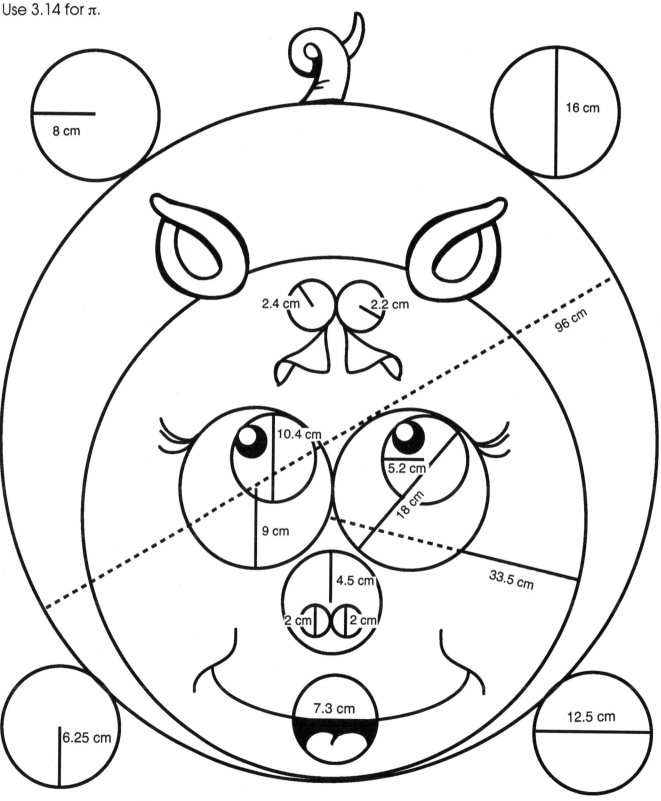

Area

Name _____

Help Bad-Hair-Day Bob get to his gel by shading in the boxes that contain the correct areas of the circles and connecting these shaded boxes. Then, find the correct areas for the ones that are wrong. Use 3.14 for π.

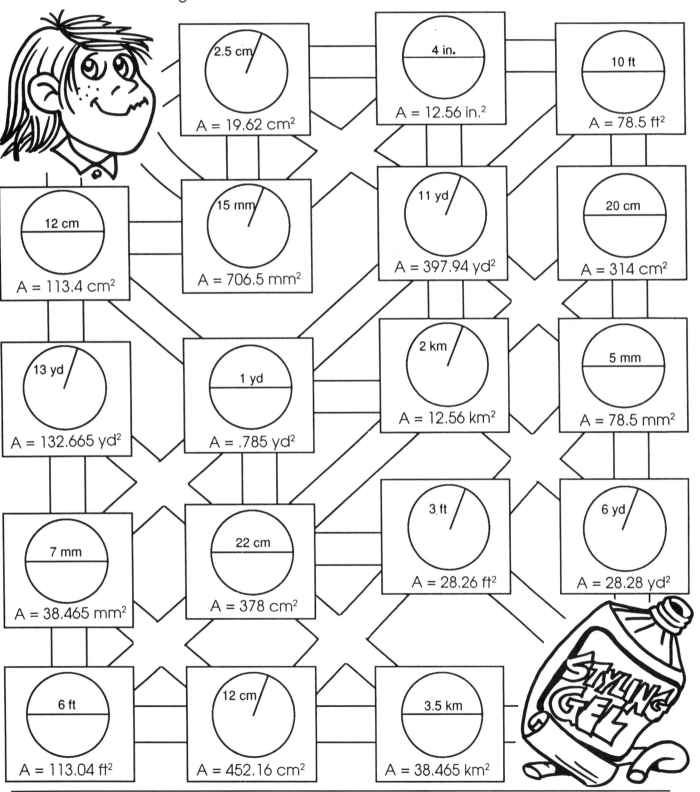

Math IF8748

©Instructional Fair, Inc.

Area

Name _____

Find the area of each circle. Use 3.14 for π.

1.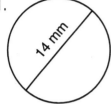
14 mm

2.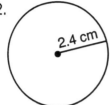
2.4 cm

3.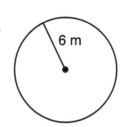
6 m

4.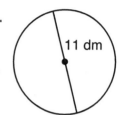
11 dm

5.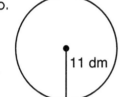
11 dm

6.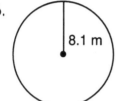
8.1 m

7.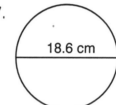
18.6 cm

8.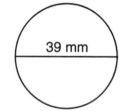
39 mm

9.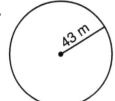
43 m

10.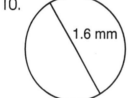
1.6 mm

11.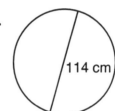
114 cm

12.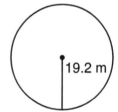
19.2 m

13.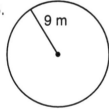
9 m

14.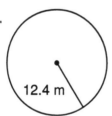
12.4 m

15.
22 mm

16.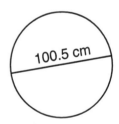
100.5 cm

17. r = 16 cm

18. r = 9.9 m

19. d = 25 dm

20. r = 14.1 cm

21. d = 2.2 mm

22. d = 158 m

23. r = 36.7 cm

24. r = 22 mm

25. r = 100 m

26. d = 8.8 mm

27. d = 5.2 cm

28. r = 97 mm

Surface Area

Name _____

Who won the first World Series in 1903?

To find out, find the surface areas of the following figures. Then, find the answers at the bottom of the page and put the corresponding letter above each answer.

S.
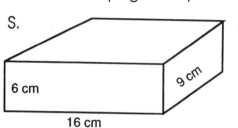
6 cm   9 cm   16 cm

D.
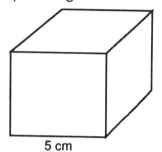
5 cm

N.
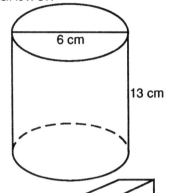
6 cm   13 cm

O.
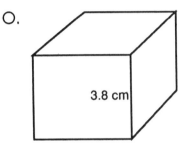
3.8 cm

O.
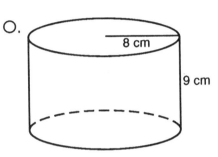
8 cm   9 cm

O.
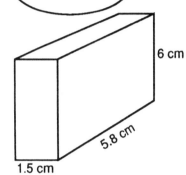
6 cm   5.8 cm   1.5 cm

E.
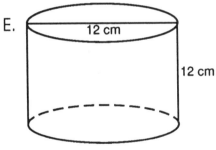
12 cm   12 cm

S.
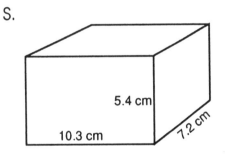
5.4 cm   10.3 cm   7.2 cm

B.
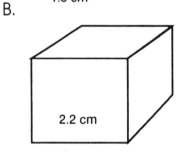
2.2 cm

R.
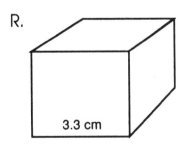
3.3 cm

X.
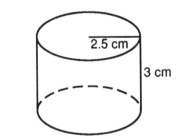
2.5 cm   3 cm

T.
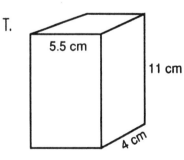
5.5 cm   11 cm   4 cm

| 29.04 cm² | 105 cm² | 588 cm² | 253 cm² | 854.08 cm² | 301.44 cm² |

| 65.34 cm² | 678.24 cm² | 150 cm² | | 337.32 cm² | 86.64 cm² | 86.35 cm² |

Surface Area

Find the surface area of each figure. Use 3.14 for π.

Name _____

1.
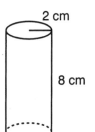
2 cm
8 cm

2.
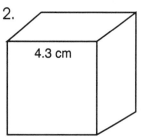
4.3 cm

3.
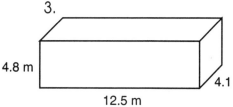
4.8 m
12.5 m
4.1 m

4.

2.1 mm

5.
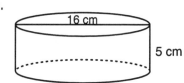
16 cm
5 cm

6.
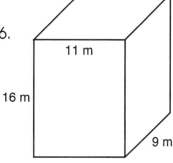
11 m
16 m
9 m

7.
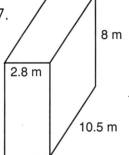
8 m
2.8 m
10.5 m

8.
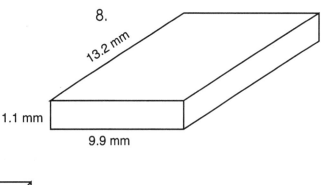
13.2 mm
1.1 mm
9.9 mm

9.
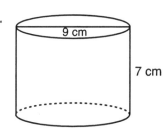
9 cm
7 cm

10.
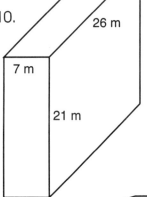
26 m
7 m
21 m

11.
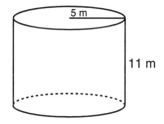
5 m
11 m

12.
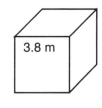
3.8 m

13.
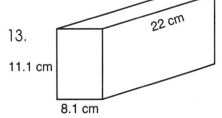
22 cm
11.1 cm
8.1 cm

14.
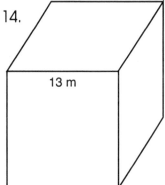
13 m

15.
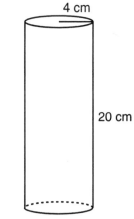
4 cm
20 cm

Surface Area

Name _____

| Why didn't the elephant buy a Corvette? |

To find out, find the surface area for each figure. Then, find the answer at the bottom of the page and put the corresponding letter above each answer.

E.
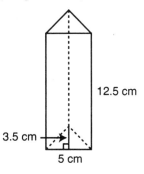
12.5 cm
3.5 cm →
5 cm

N.

9 cm
11.2 cm

P.
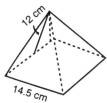
12 cm
14.5 cm

R.
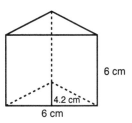
6 cm
4.2 cm
6 cm

O.
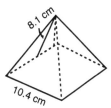
8.1 cm
10.4 cm

A.
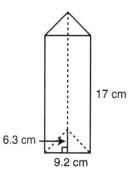
17 cm
6.3 cm →
9.2 cm

T.
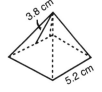
3.8 cm
5.2 cm

N.
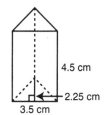
4.5 cm
2.25 cm
3.5 cm

S.
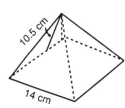
10.5 cm
14 cm

U.
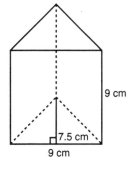
9 cm
7.5 cm
9 cm

C.

8.5 cm
11.1 cm

K.
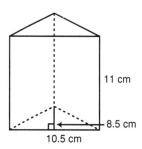
11 cm
8.5 cm
10.5 cm

_____   _____   _____   _____   _____   _____   _____

55.125 cm²   276.64 cm²   66.56 cm²   133.2 cm²   310.5 cm²   327.04 cm²   435.75 cm²

            _____   _____   _____   _____   _____

            490 cm²   558.25 cm²   527.16 cm²   311.91 cm²   205 cm²

Surface Area

Name _____

Find the surface area of each figure.

1.
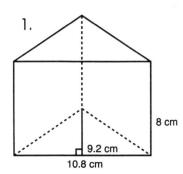
8 cm
9.2 cm
10.8 cm

2.

3 cm
2.6 cm

3.
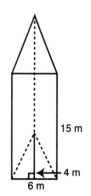
15 m
4 m
6 m

4.

17.2 cm
15.4 cm

5.
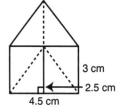
3 cm
2.5 cm
4.5 cm

6.

11.7 m
8 m

7.
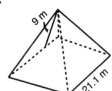
9 m
21.1 m

8.
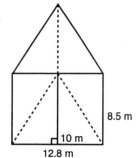
8.5 m
10 m
12.8 m

9.
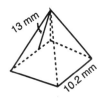
13 mm
10.2 mm

10.
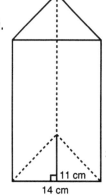
22.5 cm
11 cm
14 cm

11.
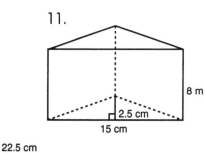
8 m
2.5 cm
15 cm

12.
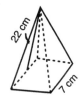
22 cm
7 cm

13.
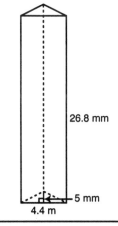
26.8 mm
5 mm
4.4 m

14.

54.4 m
21.5 m

15.
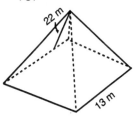
22 m
13 m

16.
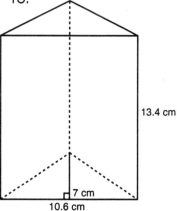
13.4 cm
7 cm
10.6 cm

Volume

Name _____

What famous portrait was painted by Humphrey Bogart's mother?

To find out, find the volumes of the following shapes. Then, find the answer at the bottom of the page and put the corresponding letter above each answer. Use 3.14 for π.

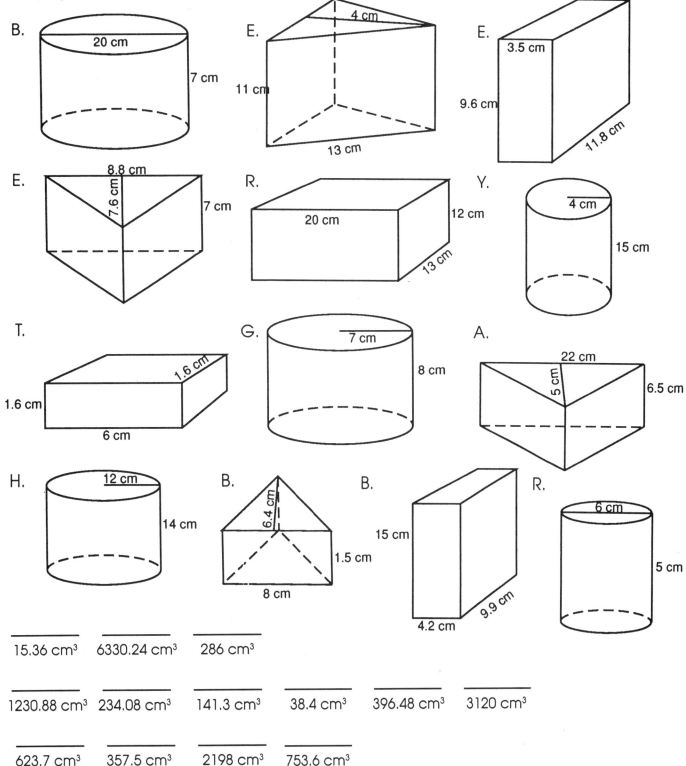

15.36 cm³   6330.24 cm³   286 cm³

1230.88 cm³   234.08 cm³   141.3 cm³   38.4 cm³   396.48 cm³   3120 cm³

623.7 cm³   357.5 cm³   2198 cm³   753.6 cm³

Volume

Name _____

Find the volume of each prism and cylinder. Use 3.14 for π.

1.
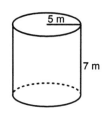

2.
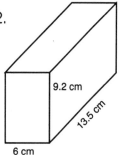

3.
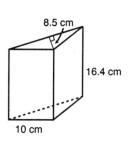

4.
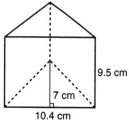

5.
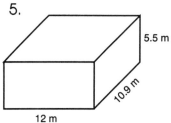

6.
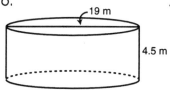

7.
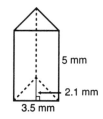

8.
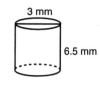

9.
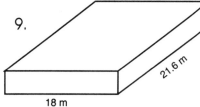

10.
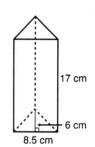

11.
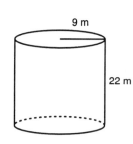

12.
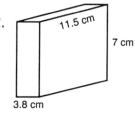

16.

13.
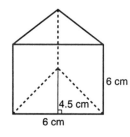

14.
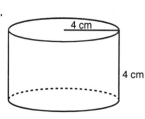

15.
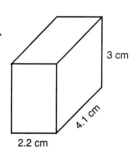

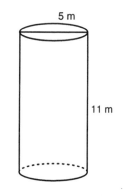

17. Triangular prism:
base area =
7.5 mm²
h = 9 mm

18. Cylinder:
d = 6 cm
h = 11 cm

19. Rectangular
prism:
l = 4 m
w = 5.6 m
h = 7.4 m

20. Cylinder:
r = 2.5 mm
h = 2 mm

21. Rectangular
prism:
l = 18.5 m
w = 16 m
h = 11.8 m

22. Triangular prism:
base area =
41.2 cm²
h = 4.5 cm

23. Cylinder:
r = 10 m
h = 17 m

24. Rectangular
prism:
l = 12.5 cm
w = 14.5 cm
h = 4 cm

Volume

Name _____

A crazy law in Charleston, South Carolina, requires all horses that pull carriages to do what?

To find out, find the volume of each shape. Then, find the answer at the bottom of the page and put the corresponding letter above each answer. Use 3.14 for π and round to the nearest hundredth.

A.
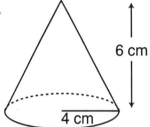
6 cm
4 cm

A.
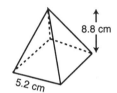
8.8 cm
5.2 cm

E.
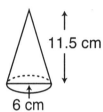
11.5 cm
6 cm

S.
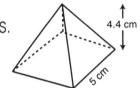
4.4 cm
5 cm

R.
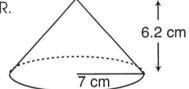
6.2 cm
7 cm

P.
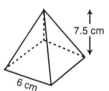
7.5 cm
6 cm

D.
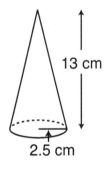
13 cm
2.5 cm

E.
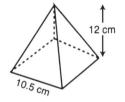
12 cm
10.5 cm

W.
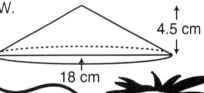
4.5 cm
18 cm

R.
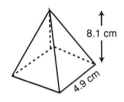
8.1 cm
4.9 cm

I.
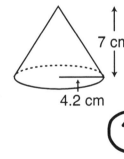
7 cm
4.2 cm

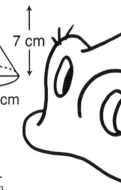

381.51 cm³	441 cm³	79.32 cm³	317.98 cm³

85.04 cm³	129.24 cm³	100.48 cm³	90 cm³	108.33 cm³	64.83 cm³	36.67 cm³

Volume

Name _____

Find the volume of each pyramid and cone. Use 3.14 for π and round to the nearest hundredth.

1.
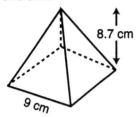
8.7 cm
9 cm

2.
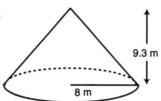
9.3 m
8 m

3.
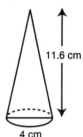
11.6 cm
4 cm

4.
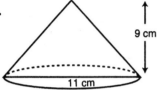
9 cm
11 cm

5.
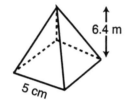
6.4 m
5 cm

6.
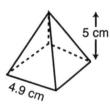
5 cm
4.9 cm

7.
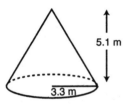
5.1 m
3.3 m

8.
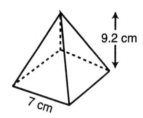
9.2 cm
7 cm

9.
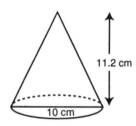
11.2 cm
10 cm

10.
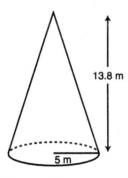
13.8 m
5 m

11.
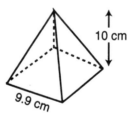
10 cm
9.9 cm

12.
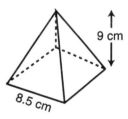
9 cm
8.5 cm

13. Pyramid:
area of base = 98 m
h = 11 m

14. Cone:
d = 12 m
h = 10.5 m

15. Cone:
r = 5.5 cm
h = 6 cm

16. Cone:
r = 3.4 cm
h = 8.1 cm

17. Pyramid:
area of base = 27.5 mm
h = 7 mm

18. Pyramid:
area of base = 42.25 cm
h = 9.8 cm

Capacity

Name _____

When one is honored as "Dentist of the Year," what does he/she get?

To find out, find the capacity for each figure. Then, find the answer at the bottom of the page and put the corresponding letter above each answer. Use 3.14 for π and round to the nearest hundredth.

A.
8.1 cm
4 cm

T.
3 cm
6.2 cm
5.5 cm

E.
3 cm
6 cm

I.
9.5 cm
7.6 cm

A.
12.5 cm
7 cm
12 cm

E.
2.1 cm
10.2 cm
13 cm

L.
12 cm
11 cm

T.
5 cm
6.1 cm

U.
9.8 cm
6 cm
7.2 cm

L.
9.9 cm
11 cm

Q.
8 cm
8.3 cm

L.
7.2 cm
6.4 cm

P.
7.7 cm
2.8 cm
3 cm

525 mL _____ 308.67 mL 182.91 mL 119.71 mL 102.3 mL 399.3 mL 278.46 mL

64.68 mL 379.94 mL 135.65 mL 183.71 mL 211.68 mL 169.56 mL

Capacity

Name _____

Find the capacity for each figure. Use 3.14 for π and round to the nearest hundredth.

1.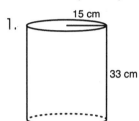
15 cm
33 cm

2.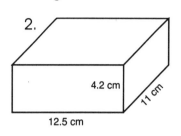
4.2 cm
11 cm
12.5 cm

3.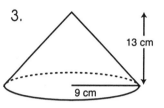
13 cm
9 cm

4.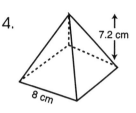
7.2 cm
8 cm

5.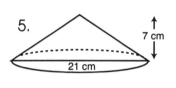
7 cm
21 cm

6.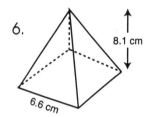
8.1 cm
6.6 cm

7.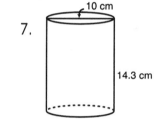
10 cm
14.3 cm

8.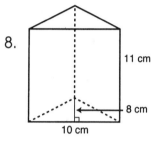
11 cm
8 cm
10 cm

9.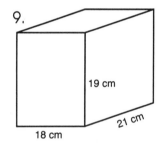
19 cm
21 cm
18 cm

10.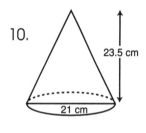
23.5 cm
21 cm

11.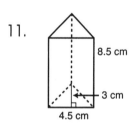
8.5 cm
3 cm
4.5 cm

12.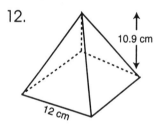
10.9 cm
12 cm

13.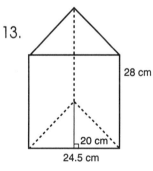
28 cm
20 cm
24.5 cm

14.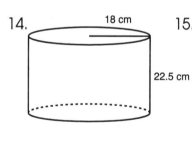
18 cm
22.5 cm

15.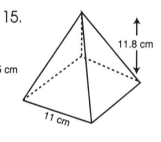
11.8 cm
11 cm

16.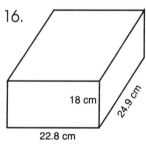
18 cm
24.9 cm
22.8 cm

17.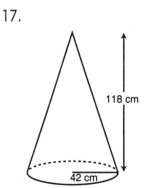
118 cm
42 cm

18.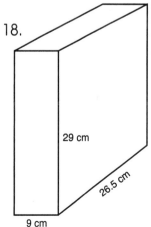
29 cm
26.5 cm
9 cm

19.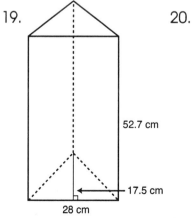
52.7 cm
17.5 cm
28 cm

20.
12 cm
42 cm

Mixed Practice

Name _____

1. Find the circumference. Use 3.14 for π.

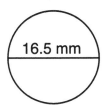

16.5 mm

2. Find the volume.

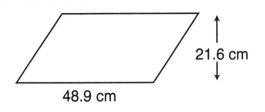

3 cm
20 cm
21.5 cm

3. Find the area.

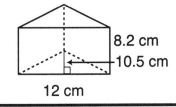

21.6 cm
48.9 cm

4. Find the surface area.

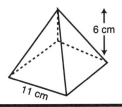

8.2 cm
-10.5 cm
12 cm

5. Find the volume and capacity.

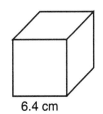

6 cm
11 cm

6. Find the surface area.

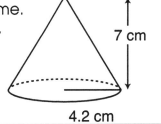

6.4 cm

7. Find the surface area. Use 3.14 for π.

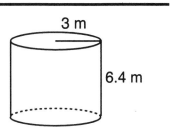

3 m
6.4 m

8. Find the perimeter.

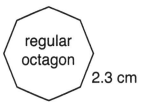

regular octagon
2.3 cm

9. Find the capacity. Use 3.14 for π.

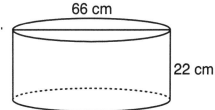

66 cm
22 cm

10. Find the area. Use 3.14 for π.

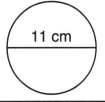

11 cm

11. Find the area.

8 mm
14.3 mm

12. Find the volume. Use 3.14 for π.

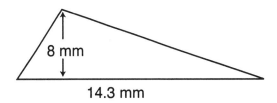

7 cm
4.2 cm

The Basic Counting Principle

Name _____

In Eureka, NV, it is against the law for a man to habitually kiss others if he has what?

To find out, use the basic counting principle to find the answers to the following questions. Find the answers at the bottom of the page and put the corresponding letter above each answer.

GOOD CHOW DINER MENU

H. pizza crust: wheat, white
toppings: pepperoni, onion, mushrooms, sausage, olives, hamburger, green pepper
How many different one-topping pizzas are possible?

U. tortilla: flour, corn, blue corn
fillings: guacamole, bean, beef, chicken, cheese, chili
How many different one-filling burritos are possible?

S. main dishes: hamburger, hot dog, grilled cheese, meat loaf
side dishes: mashed potatoes, cole slaw, French fries, cottage cheese
How many different meals are possible?

M. soups: French onion, clam chowder, chicken noodle, split pea, vegetable
salads: house, Caesar, chef, cobb, pasta
How many different soup and salad combinations are possible?

A. bread: rye, wheat, white, French, sourdough, pumpernickel
fillings: corned beef, ham, chicken salad, roast beef, salami
How many different sandwiches are possible?

A. pasta: penne, angel hair, linguini, gnachi, shells
sauce: marinara, alfredo, clam sauce
How many different pasta and sauce combinations are possible?

C. bagels: egg, plain, onion, garlic
cream cheese: plain, vegetable, pineapple, chive, strawberry, lox
How many different bagel and cream cheese combinations are possible?

E. omelettes: Californian, Western, Spanish, Cheese Lover
fruit: grapefruit, canteloupe, bananas, oranges, blueberries
How many different omelette and fruit combinations are possible?

T. yogurt: vanilla, chocolate, strawberry
toppings: M&M's, hot fudge, pineapple, caramel, granola, Oreo cookie, raspberry
How many different yogurt and topping combinations are possible?

___ ___ ___ ___ ___ ___ ___ ___
30   25   18   16   21   15   24   14   20

64

Permutations

Name _____

Who brings presents to the dentist?

Find the answers to the following sentences at the bottom of the page. Put the corresponding letter above each answer to answer the question above.

S. If 5 cars are selected from 8 and arranged side-by-side in a parking lot, how many permutations are possible?

N. How many 3-digit numbers are there using 2, 4, 6, 8 and 9?

O. How many arrangements are possible with the numbers 3, 4, 8, 9, 11 and 13?

A. How many ways can 7 horses finish win, place and show?

L. How many permutations are there of Annabella, Jake, Sophie, Ellie, Cole, Josie and Miles?

A. How many 2-digit numbers are there using 1, 2, 3, 4, 5, 6, 7, 8 and 9?

S. If 3 books are selected from 11 books and stacked on top of each other, how many arrangements are possible?

T. Jill was making out her class schedule and was interested in math, science, home economics, art, English, French, history and drama. Since she can only take 6 classes, how many arrangements are possible?

S. How many permutations are there of jack, queen, king and ace?

F. How many arrangements are possible with the letters A, B, C, D, E, F, G and H?

24	210	60	20,160	72

40,320	5,040	720	6,720	990

65

Permutations

Answer the following questions.

Name _____

1. When Larry asked Abby for her phone number, she wasn't sure if she wanted him to have it. So Abby told Larry that the prefix was 975 and that she couldn't quite remember the last digits but that they were 0, 2, 3, 6, 7, 9. How many possible phone numbers had Abby given Larry to try?

2. Sam had 9 sweaters. If he wore one a day for a week, how many permutations are possible?

3. How many arrangements are possible using 5 of the letters S, B, R, T, A, D, M, U and L?

4. How many ways can 11 runners come in first, second and third?

5. How many permutations are there of Janie, Justin, Jack, Julie, Joe, Jeff and Joanna?

6. How many 4-digit numbers are there using the numbers 0, 1, 2, 3, 4, 5, 6, 7, 8 and 9?

7. Ellie was making out her class schedule and was interested in Spanish, English, gym, typing, math, biology, social studies and art. How many different arrangements are possible if she can only take 5 classes?

8. How many permutations are there of yellow, green, blue, purple, red and orange?

9. In how many different orders can the 8 runners finish the marathon if there are no ties?

10. Bettie bought 10 pillows to try on her couch. She only wanted to keep 4 of them. How many different arrangements were possible?

Combinations

Name _____

Whose birth name was Leslie Lynch King, Jr?

To find out, find the number of combinations of the following. Then, find the answer at the bottom of the page and put the corresponding letter above the answer.

A.   4 cats from a group of 6

N.   5 songs from the top 10

O.   3 shirts from 7 shirts

E.   6 letters from T, B, M, W, L, D, J, A

E.   4 people from a group of 11

I.   2 sack lunches from a group of 13

L.   5 wolves from a pack of 8

D.   8 students from a class of 15

D.   7 sweaters from a stack of 12

R.   3 puppies from a litter of 9

R.   5 teachers from a conference of 13

R.   4 piglets from a barn of 8

E.   15 cars from a lot of 18

F.   5 kittens from a litter of 9

T.   4 doughnuts from a dozen

P.   6 letters from A, B, C, D, E, F, G, H, I, J

D.   11 necklaces from a jewelry box of 16

R.   7 songs from the top 10

S.   3 books from a stack of 6

G.   5 states from 11

210	1,287	330	20	78	6,435	816	252	495

462	28	84	15	56	4,368	70	126	35	120	792

Combinations

Find the number of combinations.

Name _____

1. 6 songs from the top 10

2. 7 dresses from a rack of 13

3. 9 doughnuts from a dozen

4. 5 puppies from a litter of 15

5. 6 states from 9 states

6. 2 letters from A, B, C, D, E, F, G, H

7. 3 kittens from a litter of 7

8. 11 cars from a lot of 20

9. 6 students from a class of 14

10. 8 sweaters from a pile of 11

11. 10 people from a group of 13

12. 5 letters from A, B, C, D, E, F, G, H

13. 14 stores from a mall of 18

14. 5 students from a class of 16

15. 4 finalists out of 17 contenders

16. 13 cars from a lot of 17

17. 3 colors from red, yellow, blue, green, purple, orange

18. 9 wolves from a pack of 14

19. 7 numbers from 1, 2, 3, 4, 5, 6, 7, 8, 9

20. 3 songs from the top 10

21. 16 students from a class of 20

22. 7 doughnuts from a dozen

23. 12 stores from a mall of 25

24. 10 dresses from a rack of 16

25. 8 songs from the top 10

26. 11 states from 18

27. 4 doughnuts from a dozen

28. 7 puppies from a litter of 11

29. 4 letters from T, U, V, W, X, Y, Z

30. 8 books from a stack of 15

68

Pascal's Triangle

Name _____

Finish Pascal's Triangle through row 15.

row 0   1

row 1   1   1

row 2   1   2   1

row 3   1   3   3   1

row 4   1   4   6   4   1

row 5   1   5   10   10   5   1

row 6   1   16   15   20   15   6   1

row 7   1   7   21   35   35   21   7   1

row 8   ___   ___   ___   ___   ___   ___   ___   ___   ___

row 9   ___   ___   ___   ___   ___   ___   ___   ___   ___   ___

row 10   ___   ___   ___   ___   ___   ___   ___   ___   ___   ___   ___

row 11   ___   ___   ___   ___   ___   ___   ___   ___   ___   ___   ___   ___

row 12   ___   ___   ___   ___   ___   ___   ___   ___   ___   ___   ___   ___   ___

row 13   ___   ___   ___   ___   ___   ___   ___   ___   ___   ___   ___   ___   ___   ___

row 14   ___   ___   ___   ___   ___   ___   ___   ___   ___   ___   ___   ___   ___   ___   ___

row 15   ___   ___   ___   ___   ___   ___   ___   ___   ___   ___   ___   ___   ___   ___   ___   ___

Use Pascal's Triangle to answer the following questions. Remember to begin at zero when counting across the rows.

1. How many combinations are there of 12 things taken 3 at a time?

2. How many combinations are there of 8 things taken 5 at a time?

3. How many combinations are there of 14 things taken 11 at a time?

4. How many combinations are there of 6 things taken 3 at a time?

5. How many combinations are there of 15 things taken 8 at a time?

6. How many combinations are there of 9 things taken 6 at a time?

7. How many combinations are there of 11 things taken 5 at a time?

Probability

Name _____

Find the probability for the die.

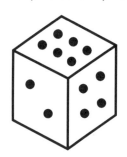

1. P (4)
2. P (odd number)
3. P (1 or 5)
4. P (multiple of 2)

5. P (prime number)
6. P (factor of 120)
7. P (8)
8. P (number < 5)

Find the probability for the spinner.

9. P (7)
10. P (2 or 3)
11. P (even number)
12. P (number > 2)
13. P (multiple of 2)
14. P (factor of 280)
15. P (odd number)
16. P (number < 5)
17. P (factor of 60)
18. P (not 5)

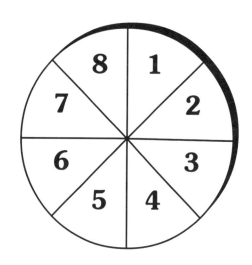

Find the probability for the spinner.

19. P (A)
20. P (C)
21. P (B or D)
22. P (A or B)
23. P (not D)
24. P (B)
25. P (C or A)
26. P (D or A)
27. P (D)
28. P (B or C)

Probability

Name _____

Think of tossing a penny and rolling a die.

1. How many events are possible?

2. What is P (H, 4)?

3. What is P (T, an even number)?

4. What is P (T, a factor of 30)?

5. What is P (H, number > 3)?

6. What is P (T, an odd number)?

7. What is P (T, not 4)?

8. What is P (H, prime number)?

9. What is P (H, 1 or 6)?

10. What is P (H, factor of 45)?

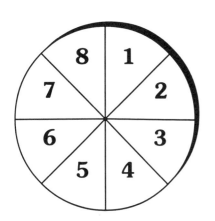

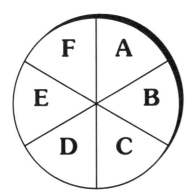

Think of spinning the two spinners.

11. How many events are possible?

12. What is P (multiple of 2, not A or D)?

13. What is P (prime number, F)?

14. What is P (7, B)?

15. What is P (2 or 3, not C)?

16. What is P (factor of 70, D or E)?

17. What is P (number < 6, A)?

18. What is P (even number, E or C or B)?

19. What is P (factor of 45, C or D)?

20. What is P (1 or 8, not F or E)?

Probability

Name _____

In Durango, CO, it is illegal for people to wear clothing in public places that is what?

To find out, predict the number of times that each event will occur. Then, find the answer at the bottom of the page. Put the corresponding letter above each answer. Round to the nearest whole number.

O. Spin the spinner
    62 times.

Event: C

E. Toss two coins
    76 times.

Event: (T, T)

N. Roll the die 97
    times.

Event: 6

I. Spin the spinners
    200 times.

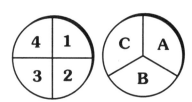

Event: (2, C)

M. Spin the spinner 65
    times.

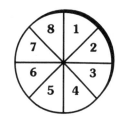

Event: number > 5

N. Spin the spinners
    650 times.

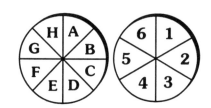

Event: (F, 5)

C. Roll the die 23
    times.

Event: factor of 20

G. Spin the spinner
    33 times.

Event: B

U. Roll the die
    77 times.

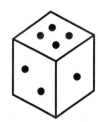

Event: multiple of 3

B. Spin the spinner
    40 times.

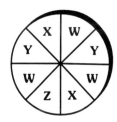

Event: not W

___ ___ ___ ___ ___ ___ ___ ___ ___ ___
26   16   25   19   15   21   24   17   14   13

Odds

Name _____

Find the odds for each event.

1. Toss both coins.

Event: both heads

odds in favor = _____

odds against = _____

2. Without looking, draw a marble from the box.

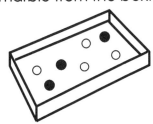

Event: drawing a white marble

odds in favor = _____

odds against = _____

3. Toss the die.

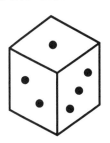

Event: factor of 12

odds in favor = _____

odds against = _____

4. Spin the spinner.

Event: getting an A

odds in favor = _____

odds against = _____

5. Toss the die.

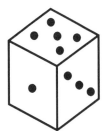

Event: number < 3

odds in favor = _____

odds against = _____

6. Spin the spinners.

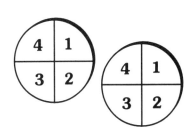

Event: sum of 7

odds in favor = _____

odds against = _____

7. Toss the dice.

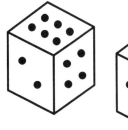 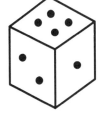

Event: sum < 6

odds in favor = _____

odds against = _____

8. Spin the spinner.

Event: even number < 7

odds in favor = _____

odds against = _____

9. Toss the dice.

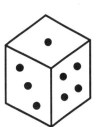 

Event: both numbers the same

odds in favor = _____

odds against = _____

Probability

Name _____

What is both small and large?

To find out, find the following probabilities. Then, find the answer at the bottom of the page and put the corresponding letter above each.

R. Draw 2 marbles without replacing them.

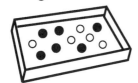

P (black, black) = _____
↑ 1st draw ↑ 2nd draw

M. Spin each spinner once.

P (odd number, even number) = _____

M. Toss a die twice.

P (5, 2) = _____

O. Spin each spinner once.

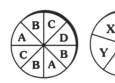

P (B, Y) = _____

U. Draw 2 cards without replacing them.

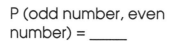

P (7, 3) = _____
↑ 1st draw ↑ 2nd draw

I. Draw 1 marble from each box.

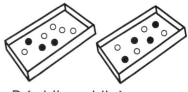

P (white, white) = _____

H. Draw 2 cards without replacing them.

P (# < 4, multiple of 4) = _____
↑ 1st draw   ↑ 2nd draw

B. Toss a die twice.

P (# > 4, # > 2) = _____

P. Draw 2 marbles without replacing them.

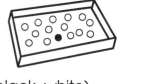

P (black, white) = _____
↑ 1st draw ↑ 2nd draw

S. Draw 2 cards without replacing them.

P (even number, even number) = _____
↑ 1st draw   ↑ 2nd draw

J. Draw 2 cards without replacing them.

P (C, C) = _____
↑ 1st draw ↑ 2nd draw

___ ___ ___ ___ ___   ___ ___ ___ ___ ___ ___
$\frac{1}{10}$ $\frac{1}{42}$ $\frac{1}{4}$ $\frac{2}{9}$ $\frac{3}{20}$ $\frac{1}{5}$ $\frac{1}{12}$ $\frac{3}{11}$ $\frac{5}{16}$ $\frac{1}{36}$ $\frac{1}{15}$

Mixed Practice

1. Finish Pascal's Triangle through row 4.

   row 0   1

   row 1   1   1

   row 2   1   2   1

   row 3   ___ ___ ___ ___

   row 4   ___ ___ ___ ___ ___

2. Main dishes: meat loaf, spaghetti, lasagne, chicken sandwich, hot dog
   side dishes: salad, mashed potatoes, French fries, corn, rice pilaf, peas
   How many different meals are possible?

3. Think of spinning the two spinners.

   What is the probability that both will be the same?

4. How many combinations of 5 doughnuts can be selected from a dozen?

5. Toss a die twice. What is P (factor of 20, odd number)?

   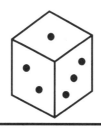

6. In how many different orders can the 9 turtles finish the race if there are no ties?

7. Give the probability.

   P (factor of 45)

   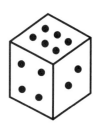

8. Predict the number of times the event will occur. Spin the spinner 120 times.
   Event: multiple of 3

9. How many different 3-digit numbers are there using 1, 2, 3, 4, 5, 6, 7, 8, 9 and 0?

10. Toss the dice.

    Event: sum of 5

    odds in favor = ____

    odds against = ____

    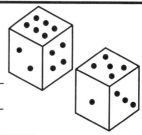

11. What is P (not X or Z)?

12. Draw 2 cards without replacing them.

    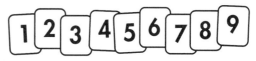

    What is P (multiple of 4, multiple of 3)?
           ↑   ↑
       1st draw   2nd draw

Tables of Data

Name _____

	Name	Period	Birth Month	State of Birth	Average Test Score
	Mrs. Miller's Math Club Members				
1.	Adams, E	5th	April	CA	96
2.	Bartlett, S.	4th	December	TX	77
3.	Campbell, B.	2nd	October	OH	88
4.	Elliot, P.	3rd	May	TX	85
5.	Flowers, V.	1st	October	MO	94
6.	Garrison, B.	3rd	November	CA	92
7.	Helton, J.	3rd	February	CA	91
8.	Lincoln, A.	4th	January	NY	80
9.	Moran, M.	5th	October	NY	90
10.	Nelson, T.	2nd	January	CA	89
11.	Ramirez, T.	2nd	November	MO	96
12.	Tam, J.	6th	December	CT	93
13.	Thomas, T.	3rd	May	MA	97
14.	Vega, S.	4th	August	VT	84
15.	Wilson, P.	6th	July	KS	98

1. Which class period has the greatest number of students as members? _____

2. What is the range of the average test scores? _____

3. Who was born in Vermont? _____

4. In what same month were three of the members born? _____

5. How many members were born in New York? _____

6. Who had the highest test average? _____

7. How many members were born in the summer (June, July, August)? _____

8. Which state has the highest frequency of members born there? _____

9. In how many states was only one member born? _____

10. Which students have average tests scores from 85 to 95? _____

    _____

11. Which average test score has the highest frequency? _____

12. In what month was T. Ramirez born? _____

13. Who was born in New York in October? _____

14. How many members have tests scores between 88 and 100? _____

15. Which class period has the lowest frequency of members? _____

Mean, Median and Mode

Name _____

Where does one go to learn Spanish?

To find out, use the tables to answer the questions below. Then, put the corresponding letter above the answer at the bottom of the page.

Chuck's Test Scores	
math	88
Spanish	73
art	94
science	84
history	73
drama	62

Boxes of Cookies Sold	
Amanda	77
Joe	111
Jill	57
Andrew	98
Molly	107
Josh	44
Terry	35
Brad	107
Sarah	66

Birth Months of Students at WJHS	
January	89
February	93
March	51
April	64
May	91
June	103
July	46
August	64
September	82
October	123
November	112
December	99

I. What is the median of boxes of cookies sold?

O. What is the mode of Chuck's scores?

E. What is the mean of students born each month?

H. What is the mode of cookies sold?

R. What is the mean of Chuck's test scores?

H. What is the mode of students born each month?

S. What is the median of Chuck's scores?

G. What is the median of students born each month?

N. What is the mean of boxes of cookies sold?

___	___	___	___	___		___	___	___	___
78.5	84.75	78	73	79		64	77	90	107

Predicting

Name _____

What do you call 500 rabbits running backwards?

Favorite Type of Pizza
Sample total: 60 students

Pizza Preferred	# of Students
pepperoni	15
sausage	12
mushroom	6
anchovy	2
Canadian bacon	10
plain	8
other	7

To find out, use the data to answer the following questions. Then, put the corresponding letter above the answer at the bottom of the page.

E. Predict the number of students out of 300 who prefer plain pizza.

E. What fraction of the 50 students buy alternative music?

E. Predict the number of students out of 2,000 who purchase disco.

A. What fraction of the 60 students prefer mushroom pizza?

E. Predict the number of students out of 300 who prefer sausage pizza.

I. Predict the number of students out of 2,000 who purchase jazz music.

A. What fraction of the 60 students prefer anchovy pizza?

I. What fraction of the 50 students buy rock-n-roll music?

D. What fraction of the 60 students prefer Canadian bacon pizza?

Type of Music Purchased
Sample total: 50 students

Variety of Music	# of Students
rap	7
rock-n-roll	12
blues	4
jazz	3
classical	1
alternative	10
country & western	2
disco	5
other	6

H. Predict the number of students out of 2,000 who purchase country and western music.

L. Predict the number of students out of 300 who prefer pepperoni pizza.

N. What fraction of the 60 students prefer a different type of pizza?

R. Predict the number of students out of 2,000 who purchase rap music.

R. What fraction of the 50 students buy blues music?

N. Predict the number of students out of 2,000 who purchase another type of music.

G. Predict the number of students out of 300 who prefer Canadian bacon pizza.

C. What fraction of the 50 students buy classical music?

___	___	___	___	___	___	___	___	___
$1/10$	280	60	$1/50$	40	$1/6$	120	$7/60$	50

___	___	___	___	___	___	___	___
80	$1/30$	$2/25$	$1/5$	75	$6/25$	240	200

Bar Graphs and Divided Bar Graphs

Name _____

Use the graphs to answer the questions.

1. What type of pizza was purchased most often?
   _____

2. How many pizzas were purchased in all? ____

3. How many more pepperoni pizzas were purchased than plain pizzas? _____

4. 30 million of what type of pizza were sold? _____

5. How many pepperoni pizzas and sausage pizzas were sold? _____

6. Which type of pizza was purchased the least?
   _____

7. How many other varieties were sold? _____

8. How many supreme pizzas and plain pizzas were sold? _____

9. How many more rock CDs did the 8th graders buy than the 6th graders?_____

10. Seventh graders purchased the same amount of which two types of music?
    _____

11. Which type of music did the seventh and eighth graders buy the same amount of?
    _____

12. How many rap CDs were purchased by students at Bedrock Middle School? _____

13. How many more rap CDs did the 8th graders purchase than alternative CDs?
    _____

14. Which grade bought 40 rock CDs? _____

PIZZAS PURCHASED

(Bar graph: Number of Pizzas (in millions) vs Type of Pizza — pepperoni 45, mushroom 30, sausage 35, plain 27, supreme 50, other 42)

15. How many alternative CDs did the 8th graders buy? _____

16. The 6th graders bought 10 CDs of which type of music? _____

17. The students at Bedrock bought 140 CDs of what type of music?
    _____

18. Which grade bought the most CDs?
    _____

19. How many CDs were purchased in all?
    _____

20. How many other types of CDs did the students buy? _____

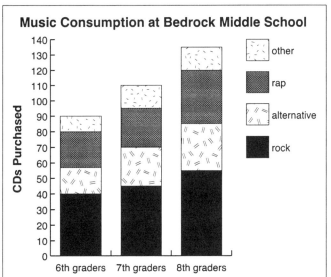

Music Consumption at Bedrock Middle School

79

Pictographs

Name _____

Use the graph to answer the questions.

Time Spent Listening to Music

Adults   🕐 🕐 🕐 🕐 🕐 🕐 🕐 🕐 🕐

Teens   🕐 🕐 🕐 🕐 🕐 🕐 🕐 🕐 🕐 🕐 🕐 🕐

Children 🕐 🕐 🕐 🕐

Each 🕐 represents 20 million hours.

1. How much time does each clock represent? _____

2. How many hours do teens spend listening to music? _____

3. How many more hours do adults listen to music than children? _____

4. Which age group listens to 170 million hours of music? _____

5. How many hours do all age groups listen to music combined? _____

6. How many facial tissues does each symbol represent? _____

7. In which year were 250 billion facial tissues used? _____

8. How many facial tissues were used in 1990? _____

9. How many facial tissues were used in 1980 and 1985? _____

10. Which two years had the same facial tissue usage? _____

11. In which year were the largest number of facial tissues used? _____

12. In which year were 225 billion facial tissues used? _____

13. How many facial tissues were used from 1970 to 1990? _____

14. How many more facial tissues were used in 1990 than 1975? _____

15. In which year were the fewest number of facial tissues used? _____

Number of Facial Tissues Used

1960 👃 👃 👃 👃 👃 👃 👃

1965 👃 👃 👃 👃 👃 👃

1970 👃 👃 👃 👃 👃

1975 👃 👃 👃 👃

1980 👃 👃 👃 👃 👃

1985 👃 👃 👃 👃

1990 👃 👃 👃 👃 👃 👃

1995 👃 👃 👃 👃 👃 👃

Each 👃 represents 50 billion tissues.

Circle Graphs

Name _____

Use the graphs to answer the questions.

DAILY STUDYING TIME

1. What percent of students study less than one hour per day? _____

2. How many hours do 40% of the students study per day? _____

3. What percent of students study 1-3 hours per day? _____

4. If 400 students were surveyed, how many would study 3 or more hours per day? _____

5. If 550 students were surveyed, how many would study 2-3 hours per day? _____

6. What percent of students study more than one hour per day? _____

7. What percent of those surveyed prefer Boyz II Men? _____

8. Six percent of those surveyed prefer who? _____

9. Which artists are preferred by the same percent of people? _____

10. What percent prefer Madonna and REM? _____

11. What percent prefer Guns N' Roses and other artists? _____

12. If 200 people were surveyed, how many would prefer REM? _____

13. If 300 people were surveyed, how many would prefer Salt-n-Pepa and Pearl Jam? _____

14. If 700 people were surveyed, how many would prefer Boyz II Men over Guns N' Roses? _____

MUSICAL ARTIST PREFERENCE

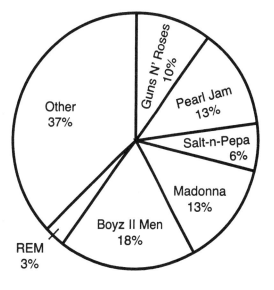

81

Line Graphs

Name _____

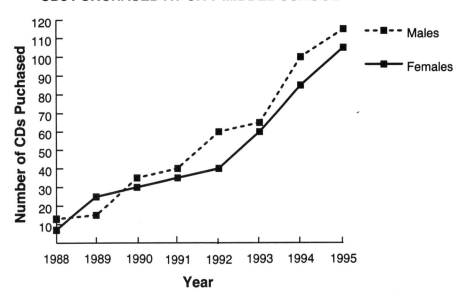

CDs PURCHASED AT CITY MIDDLE SCHOOL

1. In 1990, how many CDs did the female students buy? _____

2. In which year did the male students purchase 40 CDs? _____

3. How many CDs did the male students buy in 1993? _____

4. In which year(s) did the females buy more CDs than the males? _____

5. In which year(s) did the male students purchase five more CDs than the female students? _____

6. How many more CDs did the male students buy than the female students in 1994? _____

7. How many CDs did the female students buy between 1990 and 1993? _____

8. In which year did the female students buy 40 CDs? _____

9. How many fewer CDs did the female students buy than the male students in 1990? _____

10. How many CDs did the male and female students purchase in 1995? _____

11. How many fewer CDs did the male students buy in 1991 than in 1995? _____

12. In which year did the students buy 125 CDs? _____

13. How many CDs did the students at City Middle School purchase in 1991? _____

14. How many more CDs did the females buy in 1993 than in 1989? _____

15. In which year did the students buy 185 CDs? _____

16. What is the difference in the total number of CDs purchased by students in 1989 and 1990? _____

Scattergrams

Name _____

State if the following scattergrams show a positive correlation, negative correlation or no correlation.

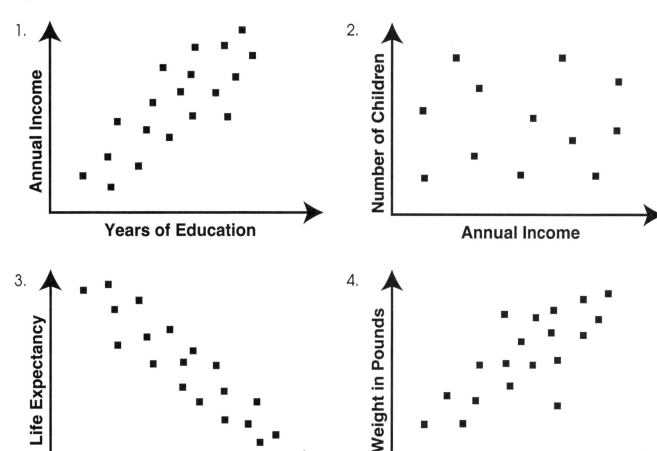

1. Annual Income vs. Years of Education

2. Number of Children vs. Annual Income

3. Life Expectancy vs. Cigarettes Smoked Per Day

4. Weight in Pounds vs. Daily Calorie Intake

State the type of correlation each of the following would have if put into a scattergram.

5. Age of car and resale value _____

6. Number of pets in household and number of fleas _____

7. Height and life expectancy _____

8. Annual income and square footage of home _____

9. Hours of TV watched and grades _____

10. Weight and annual income _____

11. Age and number of health problems _____

12. Hours of exercise per day and weight _____

Stem and Leaf Plots

Name _____

The weights of all of the babies born at Infantville Hospital on January 13th, 1995 were recorded in ounces as follows: 101, 128, 112, 105, 96, 88, 132, 139, 97, 115, 105, 147, 138, 96, 122, 133, 107, 122, 129, 111, 119, 122, 136, 148, 125, 139 and 124.

Stem	Leaf

1. Put the data in the stem and leaf plot.

2. Use the stem and leaf plot to name the value repeated three times. _____

3. Which three values are repeated twice?

   _____

4. Were most babies born below or above 120 ounces? _____

5. Are there more values with a stem of 12 or a stem of 13? _____

6. Which stem has three values? _____

The ages of all the guests at Ellie's 40th Birthday Bash were recorded as follows: 52, 41, 26, 38, 40, 62, 55, 43, 48, 57, 39, 37, 45, 70, 56, 64, 29, 50, 61, 73, 28, 44, 53, 41, 55, 67, 42, 36, 26, 35, 40, 53, 63, 26 and 41.

7. Put the data in the stem and leaf plot.

8. How many leaves does the stem 5 have?

   _____

9. How many times does the age 64 appear?

   _____

Stem	Leaf

10. Which age occurs more frequently, 55 or 26? _____

11. Which stem has the most values?

    _____

12. Which stems have 5 values?

    _____

13. Were most of the guests younger or older than 50? _____

14. Which values appear more than once? _____

84

Frequency Tables and Histograms

Name _____

Dinner Sales at Spametria						
$18.78	$19.25	$ 1.99	$10.00	$ 3.33	$19.15	$ 5.60
$12.92	$11.90	$16.21	$14.88	$ 8.26	$11.29	$ 8.88
$6.18	$13.16	$ 9.56	$ 9.21	$15.20	$15.16	$18.14
$7.56	$ 8.46	$13.99	$17.52	$ 2.85	$18.99	$12.65
$11.11	$ 4.91	$17.78	$16.29	$ .99	$ 7.12	$10.48

1. Make a stem and leaf plot that represents the 35 dinner sales. Use the dollars as stems and the cents as leaves.

2. Using this stem and leaf plot, complete the frequency table.

Stem	Leaf

Frequency Table

Grouping Intervals	Frequency
0-$4.99	
$5.00 - $9.99	
$10.00 - $14.99	
$15.00 - $19.99	

3. Use this frequency table to complete the histogram.

4. Using the stem and leaf plot (#1), construct a frequency table with $4.00 intervals.

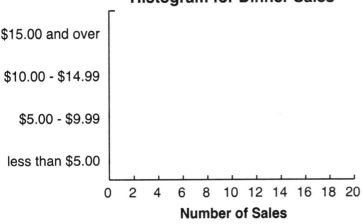

Histogram for Dinner Sales

$15.00 and over

$10.00 - $14.99

$5.00 - $9.99

less than $5.00

0 2 4 6 8 10 12 14 16 18 20

Number of Sales

5. Using the frequency table from #4, make a histogram with $4.00 intervals on the back of this page.

Box and Whisker Graphs

Name _____

Draw box and whisker graphs for the following sets of data. First, make a stem and leaf plot.

1. 96, 52, 38, 66, 72, 81, 87, 65, 48,
    91, 75, 82, 49, 56, 78, 65, 90, 71

Stem	Leaf

```
100 ┬
    │
 80 ┼
    │
 60 ┼
    │
 40 ┼
    │
 20 ┼
    │
  0 ┴
```

2. 3.2, 4.1, 3.5, 5.6, 4.2, 2.9, 7.7, 5.4, 6.1,
    6.5, 5.8, 4.7, 6.2, 2.8, 4.0, 5.1

Stem	Leaf

```
10 ┬
   │
 8 ┼
   │
 6 ┼
   │
 4 ┼
   │
 2 ┼
   │
 0 ┴
```

3. 22, 13, 40, 18, 11, 15, 25, 31, 8, 19,
    33, 20, 5, 28, 35, 16, 42, 10

Stem	Leaf

```
50 ┬
   │
40 ┼
   │
30 ┼
   │
20 ┼
   │
10 ┼
   │
 0 ┴
```

4. 3.3, 2.7, 4.9, 0.6, 1.1, 2.0, 1.5, 3.7, 1.1,
    4.2, 4.6, 2.5, 1.7, 3.4

Stem	Leaf

```
5 ┬
  │
4 ┼
  │
3 ┼
  │
2 ┼
  │
1 ┼
  │
0 ┴
```

Mixed Practice

Name _____

---

1. What type of correlation does the scattergram show?

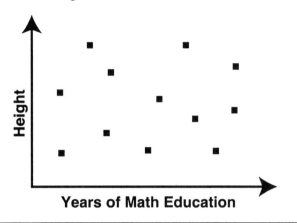

2. If 400 people were surveyed, how many would prefer Ricki Lake and Geraldo?

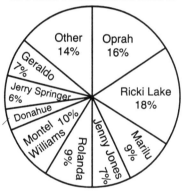

Talk Show Preference at Couch Potato Middle School

Other 14%, Oprah 16%, Geraldo 7%, Jerry Springer 6%, Donahue 4%, Montel Williams 10%, Rolanda 9%, Jenny Jones 7%, Marilu 9%, Ricki Lake 18%

3. Make a stem and leaf plot for the following data: 111, 143, 138, 126, 105, 135, 151, 127, 118, 148, 131, 139, 122, 147, 136, 144, 138, 141, 127, 112, 157.

stem	leaf

Name two values that are repeated.

4. Draw a box and whisker graph for the following set of data: 8.8, 5.3, 6.6, 7.1, 3.9, 1.8, 9.6, 6.4, 7.3, 5.5, 6.9, 8.4, 2.7, 5.2.

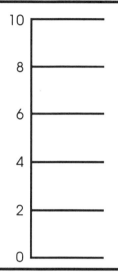

5. How many more hours were spent on the telephone in 1994 than in 1991?

Hours Spent on the Telephone

1995 ☎☎☎☎
1994 ☎☎☎☎☎☎
1993 ☎☎☎☎☎
1992 ☎☎☎☎
1991 ☎☎☎

Each ☎ represents 50 million hours.

6. How many babies were between 20" and 21" in height?

Babies Born February 14th at Rugrat Hospital

Name (Sex)	Eye Color	Height	Weight	Time
1. Hoo, B. (F)	blue	21 in.	8 lb 1 oz	1:20 a.m.
2. Smith, J. (M)	brown	20 in.	7 lb 13 oz	3:45 a.m.
3. Miles, A. (F)	green	20 1/2 in.	8 lb 13 oz	6:02 a.m.
4. Perez, T. (M)	brown	21 in.	6 lb 10 oz	12:05 p.m.
5. Jones, F. (M)	brown	18 1/2 in.	4 lb 10 oz	4:10 p.m.
6. Azideh, L. (F)	blue	19 in.	9 lb	7:22 p.m.

Mixed Practice
continued

---

7. Predict the number of students out of 600 who watched *Loving*.

Soap Operas Watched
Sample Total: 50 students

Programs Watched	# of Students
All My Children	11
General Hospital	10
The Young and the Restless	7
Loving	6
Days of Our Lives	5
Guiding Light	4
Another World	4
One Life to Live	3

10. Which program attracts the smallest female audience?

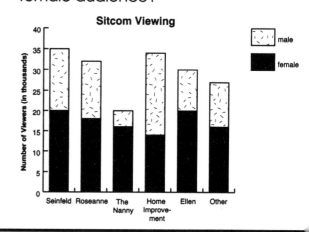

8. Make a frequency table with 10-point frequency intervals.

Test Scores of 5th Period

81	90	56	51	96	76
72	83	82	75	73	84
66	41	89	91	49	74
70	71	68	63	77	58
85	64	94	70	83	63

Grouping Intervals	Frequency	Grouping Intervals	Frequency

11. What is the mean?

Lipstick Selections

Pink Passion	61
Cute Coral	49
Marvelous Magenta	58
Buttery Brown	59
Puckering Peach	73
Outrageous Orange	38
Radical Red	60
Bodacious Beige	76

9. Using the frequency table from #8, make a histogram for this data with 10-point intervals.

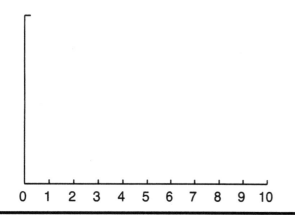

12. In what year was the male and female viewing 7 ¹/₂ hours per day?

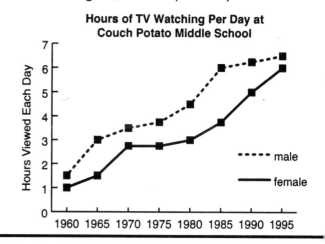

Squares and Square Roots

Name _____

Did you hear about the student that didn't like school?

To get the punchline, find the square root of each problem. Then, put the corresponding letter above each answer at the bottom of the page.

A. $-\sqrt{81}$ H. $\sqrt{64}$ T. $-\sqrt{36}$ T. $\sqrt{25}$ C. $\sqrt{49}$

N. $-\sqrt{144}$ A. $\sqrt{400}$ R. $\sqrt{121}$ H. $-\sqrt{16}$ F. $-\sqrt{100}$

E. $\sqrt{225}$ I. $-\sqrt{49}$ E. $-\sqrt{196}$ S. $\sqrt{625}$ P. $-\sqrt{1}$

I. $\sqrt{169}$ I. $-\sqrt{9}$ T. $-\sqrt{256}$ W. $\sqrt{36}$ G. $\sqrt{144}$

T. $\sqrt{10,000}$ N. $\sqrt{81}$ H. $\sqrt{100}$ L. $-\sqrt{1,600}$

O. $-\sqrt{900}$ I. $\sqrt{2,500}$ P. $-\sqrt{169}$

___ ___   ___ ___ ___   ___ ___ ___
13   5   6   20   25   -6   10   15

___ ___ ___ ___ ___ ___ ___ ___ ___
-13 11   -3   9   7   50   -1   -9   -40

___ ___   ___ ___ ___   ___ ___ ___ ___ ___ !
-30 -10   -16 8   -14   100 -4   -7   -12 12

Square Roots

Name _____

> Tulsa, OK, has an ordinance against what?

To find out, find the square roots of the numbers using the table. Then, put the letter above the square root at the bottom of the page.

Table of Squares and Square Roots

#	Square	Square Root	#	Square	Square Root
n	n^2	$\sqrt{n}$	n	n^2	$\sqrt{n}$
1	1	1.000	21	441	4.583
2	4	1.414	22	484	4.690
3	9	1.732	23	529	4.796
4	16	2.000	24	576	4.899
5	25	2.236	25	625	5.000
6	36	2.449	26	676	5.099
7	49	2.646	27	729	5.196
8	64	2.828	28	784	5.292
9	81	3.000	29	841	5.385
10	100	3.162	30	900	5.477
11	121	3.317	31	961	5.568
12	144	3.464	32	1,024	5.657
13	169	3.606	33	1,089	5.745
14	196	3.742	34	1,156	5.831
15	225	3.873	35	1,225	5.916
16	256	4.000	36	1,296	6.000
17	289	4.123	37	1,369	6.083
18	324	4.243	38	1,444	6.164
19	361	4.359	39	1,521	6.245
20	400	4.472	40	1,600	6.325

A. $\sqrt{34}$ R. $\sqrt{18}$ N. $\sqrt{22}$ S. $\sqrt{2}$

H. $\sqrt{39}$ T. $\sqrt{15}$ A. $\sqrt{5}$ R. $\sqrt{29}$

A. $\sqrt{11}$ H. $\sqrt{28}$ E. $\sqrt{37}$ T. $\sqrt{20}$

T. $\sqrt{8}$ S. $\sqrt{32}$ O. $\sqrt{26}$ R. $\sqrt{33}$

L. $\sqrt{14}$ F. $\sqrt{10}$ H. $\sqrt{19}$ S. $\sqrt{40}$

I. $\sqrt{3}$ S. $\sqrt{1}$ E. $\sqrt{12}$ E. $\sqrt{21}$

I. $\sqrt{13}$ N. $\sqrt{6}$ T. $\sqrt{30}$ M. $\sqrt{7}$

T. $\sqrt{38}$ E. $\sqrt{31}$ O. $\sqrt{27}$ T. $\sqrt{4}$

E. $\sqrt{24}$ K. $\sqrt{17}$ U. $\sqrt{35}$ M. $\sqrt{23}$

S. $\sqrt{36}$

___ ___ ___ ___ ___ ___   ___ ___ ___ ___
4.123 1.732 6 1.414 4.899 5.657   6.164 5.292 5.831 5.477

___ ___ ___ ___   ___ ___ ___   ___ ___ ___ ___
3.742 3.317 1.000 3.873   3.162 5.196 5.385   2.646 5.099 4.243 4.583

___ ___ ___ ___   ___ ___ ___ ___ ___
4.472 4.359 2.236 2.449   2 6.245 5.745 6.083 3.464

___ ___ ___ ___ ___ ___ ___
4.796 3.606 4.690 5.916 2.828 5.568 6.325

Square Roots

Name _____

What is another term for beef stew?

To find out, estimate the following square roots to the nearest hundredth using the divide and average method. Then, put the letter above each answer at the bottom of the page. Find the answer closest to your own if one is not exactly the same.

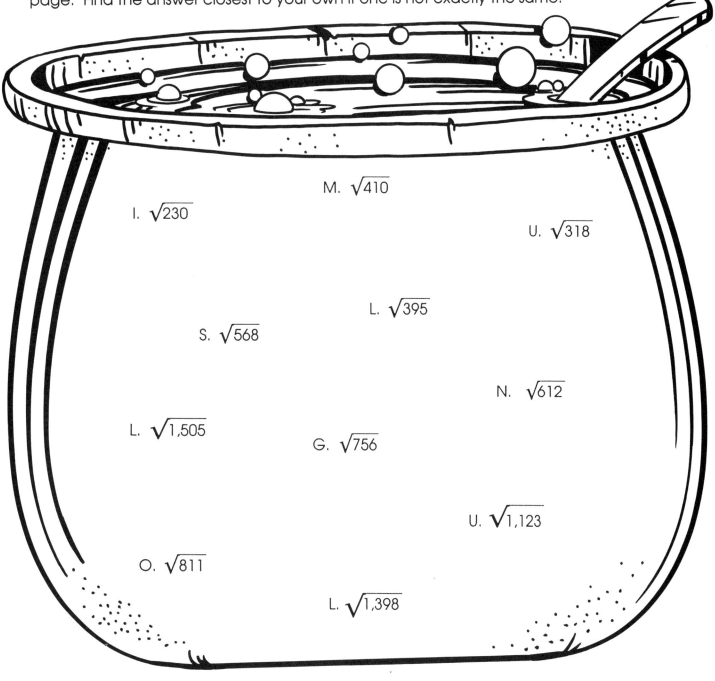

M. $\sqrt{410}$

I. $\sqrt{230}$

U. $\sqrt{318}$

L. $\sqrt{395}$

S. $\sqrt{568}$

N. $\sqrt{612}$

L. $\sqrt{1,505}$

G. $\sqrt{756}$

U. $\sqrt{1,123}$

O. $\sqrt{811}$

L. $\sqrt{1,398}$

| 23.83 | 38.79 | 33.51 | 20.25 | 27.5 | 17.84 | 37.39 | 19.88 | 15.17 | 28.48 | 24.74 |

Pythagorean Theorem

Name _____

What famous swine created the frescoes on the ceiling of the Pigstine Chapel?

To find out, use a table of square roots or a calculator to find the length of each hypotenuse to the nearest thousandth. Then, put the corresponding letter above each answer at the bottom of the page.

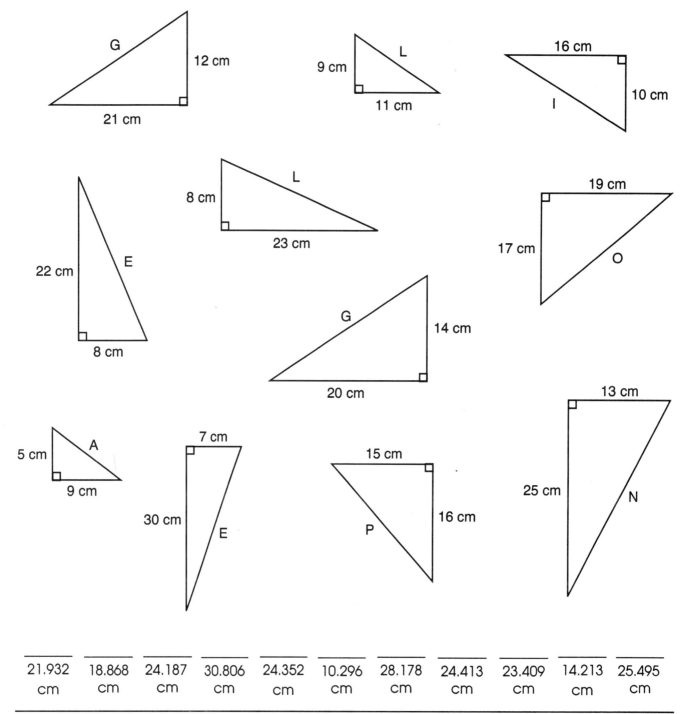

21.932 cm	18.868 cm	24.187 cm	30.806 cm	24.352 cm	10.296 cm	28.178 cm	24.413 cm	23.409 cm	14.213 cm	25.495 cm

©Instructional Fair, Inc.

Pythagorean Theorem

Name _____

| What was written on the vegetable farmer's tombstone? |

To find the punchline, use a table of square roots or a calculator to find the length of each leg not given to the nearest thousandth. Then, put the corresponding letter above each answer at the bottom of the page.

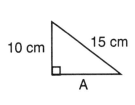

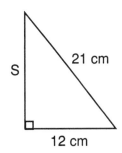

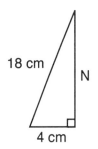

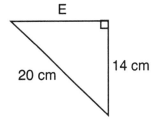

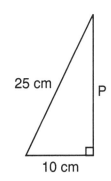

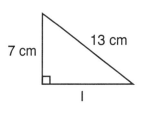

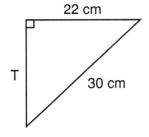

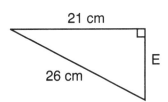

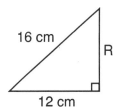

10.583 cm   14.283 cm   17.234 cm   20.396 cm   10.954 cm   17.55 cm

22.913 cm   15.33 cm   11.18 cm   6.325 cm

30°-60° Right Triangles

Name _____

It is against the law to do what when admiring a member of the opposite sex in San Antonio, TX?

To find out, find the lengths of the unknown sides of each triangle using a calculator and rounding to the nearest tenth when necessary. Locate the lengths at the bottom of the page and put the corresponding letter above each.

O: 60° / 20 cm / 30° / N

R: 60° / 6 cm / 30° / N

I: 60° / 35 cm / 30° / B

5.5 cm / 60° / W / F / 30°

13 cm: 60° / 30° / I / I / 60°

25 cm: 30° / 60° / Y / G

9.5 cm: 60° / T / L / 30°

K: 60° / I / 30 cm / 30°

19 cm	10 cm		9.5 cm	16.5 cm	22.5 cm	12 cm	26 cm

30.3 cm	21.7 cm		11 cm	26 cm	10.4 cm	15 cm	17.5 cm	17.3 cm	12.5 cm

45°-45° Right Triangles

Name _____

What happened to the girl who stole mascara?

To find out, use a calculator to find the hypotenuse of each triangle to the nearest tenth. Then, put the corresponding letter above each answer at the bottom of the page.

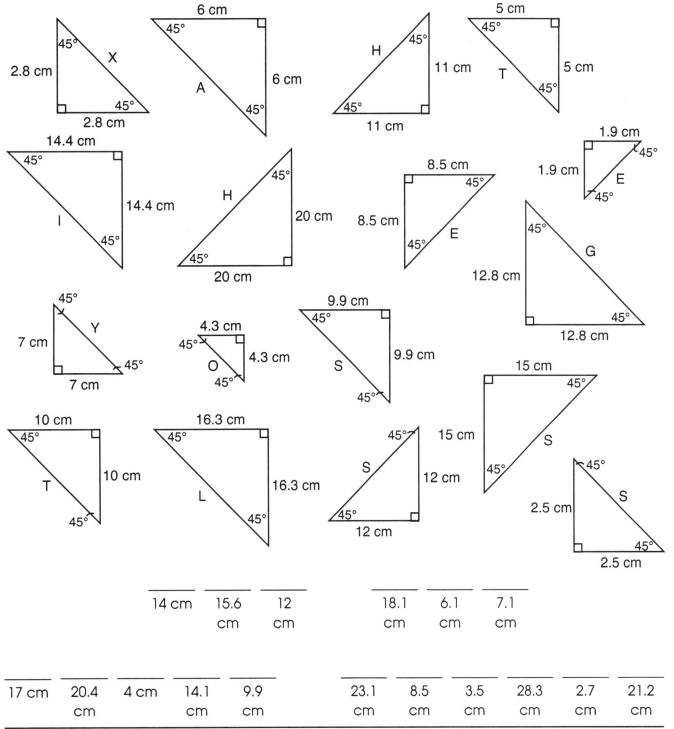

| 14 cm | 15.6 cm | 12 cm | | 18.1 cm | 6.1 cm | 7.1 cm |

| 17 cm | 20.4 cm | 4 cm | 14.1 cm | 9.9 cm | | 23.1 cm | 8.5 cm | 3.5 cm | 28.3 cm | 2.7 cm | 21.2 cm |

Sine Ratios

Name _____

What are galligaskins?

To find out, find sine A to the nearest thousandth and put the corresponding letter above the answer at the bottom of the page.

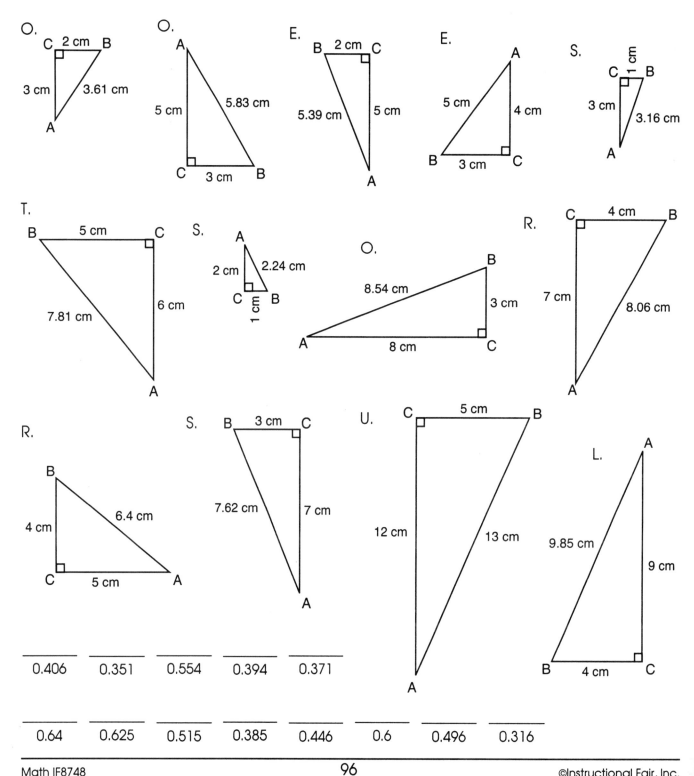

0.406	0.351	0.554	0.394	0.371

0.64	0.625	0.515	0.385	0.446	0.6	0.496	0.316

Cosine Ratios

Name _____

What is pogonotrophy?

To find out, find cos A to the nearest thousandth and put the corresponding letter above the answer at the bottom of the page.

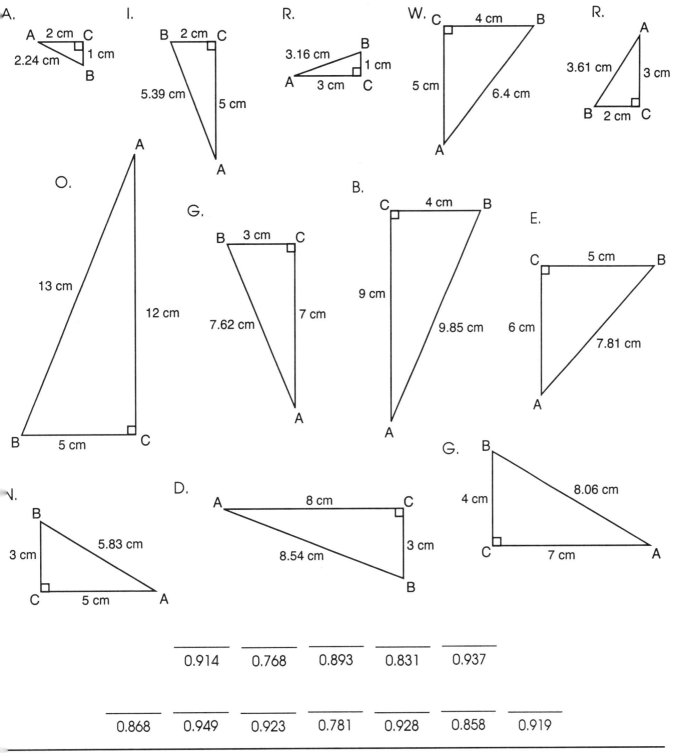

A.

A 2 cm C
2.24 cm 1 cm
B

I.

B 2 cm C
5.39 cm 5 cm
A

R.

B
3.16 cm 1 cm
A 3 cm C

W.

C 4 cm B
5 cm 6.4 cm
A

R.

A
3.61 cm 3 cm
B 2 cm C

O.

A
13 cm 12 cm
B 5 cm C

G.

B 3 cm C
7.62 cm 7 cm
A

B.

C 4 cm B
9 cm 9.85 cm
A

E.

C 5 cm B
6 cm 7.81 cm
A

N.

B
3 cm 5.83 cm
C 5 cm A

D.

A 8 cm C
8.54 cm 3 cm
B

G.

B
4 cm 8.06 cm
C 7 cm A

____ ____ ____ ____ ____
0.914 0.768 0.893 0.831 0.937

____ ____ ____ ____ ____ ____ ____
0.868 0.949 0.923 0.781 0.928 0.858 0.919

Mixed Practice

Name _____

1. Give the length of the hypotenuse to the nearest thousandth.

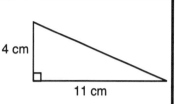
4 cm
11 cm

7. Find the hypotenuse and round to the nearest tenth.

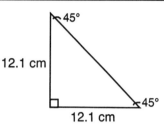
45°
12.1 cm
45°
12.1 cm

2. Using the table from page 90, find the square root.

$$\sqrt{1{,}024}$$

8. Give the square root.

$$-\sqrt{289}$$

3. Find the length of the leg to the nearest thousandth.

15 cm
6 cm

9. Find sine A to the nearest thousandth.

B
25 cm
7 cm
A
24 cm

4. Find the hypotenuse and round to the nearest tenth.

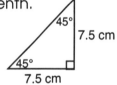
45°
7.5 cm
45°
7.5 cm

10. Find the lengths of the unknown sides and round to the nearest tenth.

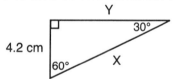
Y
30°
4.2 cm
60°
X

5. Find cos A to the nearest thousandth.

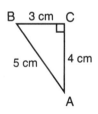
B   3 cm   C
5 cm
4 cm
A

11. Find the length of the leg to the nearest thousandth.

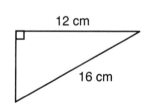
12 cm
16 cm

6. Find the lengths of the unknown sides and round to the nearest tenth.

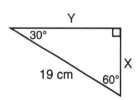
Y
30°
19 cm
60°
X

12. Estimate the square root to the nearest hundredth using the divide and average method.

$$\sqrt{135.5}$$

Cumulative Mixed Practice

Name _____

1. Draw 2 cards without replacing them.

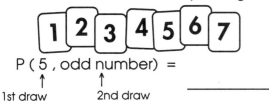

P (5 , odd number) =

↑   ↑   _____
1st draw   2nd draw

2. Find the length of the unknown sides. Round to the nearest tenth.

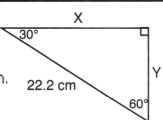

6. Add.

$$\begin{array}{r} 2 \text{ yd } 1 \text{ ft } 8 \text{ in.} \\ + \ 5 \text{ yd } 1 \text{ ft } 7 \text{ in.} \\ \hline \end{array}$$

7. Name the triangle by the length of its sides.

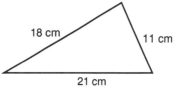

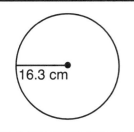

3. Find the circumference. Use 3.14 for π.

8.

Ages of People in Room					
13	8	10	16	29	2
21	1	12	13	27	11
30	14	3	9	8	22
6	20	19	4	5	23

Make a frequency table with five-year age intervals.

4. Write the missing unit.

962 mm = 0.962 _____

5. If 250 people were surveyed, how many would want 1-3 children?

Number of Children Desired

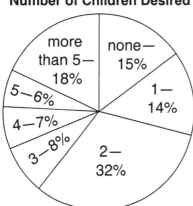

9. Make a histogram for #8 with frequency intervals of five years.

10. Write in scientific notation.

0.0000000000000005864

Cumulative Mixed Practice (continued)

Name _____

11. Find X.

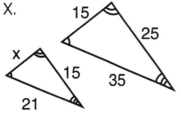

12. Find the length of the leg to the nearest thousandth.

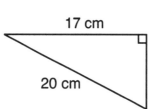

13. Solve.

$$-17 + |-28| = \underline{\hspace{2cm}}$$

14. How many combinations are possible if four people are selected from a group of eight people?

15. Susan flew from San Diego to Portland. She departed at 10:22 a.m. Pacific time and arrived at 12:05 p.m. Pacific time. How long was her flight?

16. Find the area.

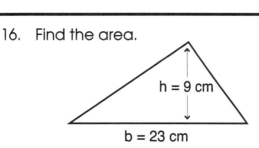

17. How many eighth graders view comedies?

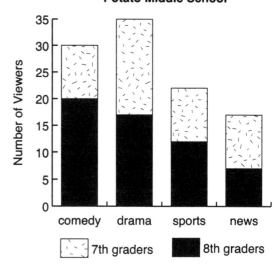

Television Viewing at Couch Potato Middle School

18. Give the missing number.

$$3a = \underline{\hspace{2cm}} ft^2$$

19. Find the surface area.

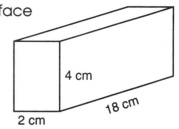

20. Find the value.

$$(2 + 5)^2 - 6 \times 5 + 4^2 \times 3 - (6^2 + 20)$$

21. Find cos A to the nearest hundredth.

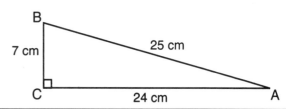

Cumulative Mixed Practice (continued)

Name _____

---

22. Give the missing number.

2.22 daL = _____ dL

23. Predict the number of people out of 900 who prefer to drink milk or soda with dinner.

Beverage Preferred With Dinner
Sample Total: 75 people

Beverage Preferred	Number of People
milk	8
water	12
soda	9
iced tea	11
coffee	14
other	21

24. Find the GCF.

144, 264

25. Find sine A to the nearest hundredth.

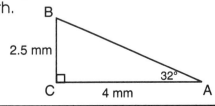

26. Give the tangent of ∠A to the nearest thousandth.

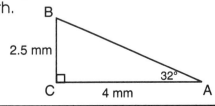

---

27. Find the volume. Use 3.14 for π.

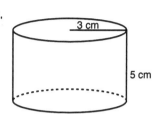

28. Give the length of the hypotenuse to the nearest thousandth.

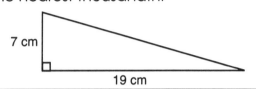

29. Find the missing number.

2 yd^3 = _____ in.^3

30. Find the probability.

P (factor of 105)

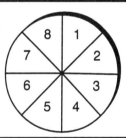

31. Write as a percent.

$5\dfrac{61}{250}$

32. Find the measure of ∠C.

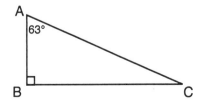

Cumulative Mixed Practice (continued)

Name _____

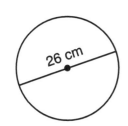

33. Find the area.
    Use 3.14 for π.

26 cm

34. Find the missing number.

    _____ c = 5 qt

35. Find the odds.

    Event: getting a
    multiple of 3

    Odds in favor = _____

    Odds against = _____

36. Find the LCM.

    30, 8

37. The numbers in Jack's phone number
    are 0, 2, 4, 5, 6, 7 and 9. How many
    possible phone numbers are there?

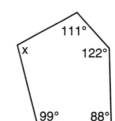

38. Find the volume.
    Use 3.14 for π.

    h = 12.5 cm

    6 cm

39. Give the prime factorization of 840.

40. Find the hypotenuse
    and round to the
    nearest tenth.

    45°
    8.9 cm
    45°
    8.9 cm

41. Draw a box and whisker graph for the
    set of data: 12, 14, 22, 38, 6, 29, 5, 28,
    37, 41, 11, 9, 18, 30.

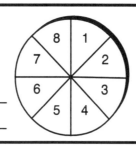

42. Find the degree
    measure of X.

    111°
    x
    122°
    99°   88°

43. Give in degrees Celsius.

    385.75 K

ANSWER KEY

Page 1

Exponents
Skill: exponential notation

Name _____

Write in exponential notation.

1. 5×5×5×5×5 5^5
2. 3•3•3•3•3•3•3 3^7
3. 11•11•11•11 11^4
4. 9•9•9•9•9•9 9^6
5. 2•2•2•2•2•2•2•2 2^8
6. 3.8×3.8 $(3.8)^2$
7. 14•14•14 14^3
8. 4×4×4×4×4 4^5
9. 100•100 100^2
10. 4.5×4.5×4.5×4.5 $(4.5)^4$
11. (0.7)(0.7)(0.7) $(0.7)^3$
12. 6•6•6•6•6•6 6^6

Write the numeral.

13. 12^2 = 144
14. 21^1 = 21
15. 2^8 = 256
16. 3^5 = 243
17. 20^3 = 8,000
18. 4^3 = 64
19. 21^2 = 441
20. 15^2 = 225
21. 5^4 = 625
22. 7^3 = 343
23. 2^6 = 64
24. 9^2 = 81
25. 2^7 = 128
26. 8^3 = 512
27. 3^4 = 81
28. 18^2 = 324
29. 33^1 = 33
30. 15^0 = 1
31. 6^3 = 216
32. 2^5 = 32
33. 50^1 = 50

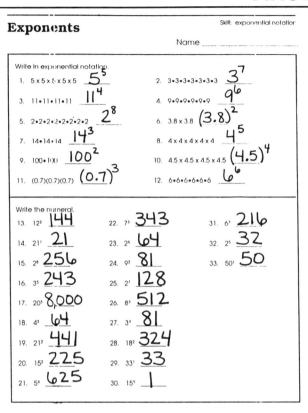

Page 1

Page 2

Exponents
Skill: multiplying and dividing exponents

Name _____

What did the duck say to the cashier?

To find out, locate the answers to the following problems at the bottom of the page. Put the letter of the problem above the corresponding answer.

L. $4^2 \cdot 4^3$
O. $12^{20} \div 12^{18}$

I. $(2.1)^{13} \div (2.1)^{11}$
U. $(9.04)^9 \div (9.04)^8$
Y. $2^3 \cdot 2^4$

P. $10^2 \cdot 10^2$
B. $5^{14} \div 5^{12}$
I. $(6.6)^{10} \div (6.6)^8$

M. $7^{17} \div 7^{14}$
S. $3^4 \times 3^2$
T. $(9.9)^1 \cdot (9.9)^1$

N. $(0.1)^3 \times (0.1)^1$
H. $8^{11} \div 8^8$

L. $(0.11)^8 \div (0.11)^8$
T. $(0.3)^2 \cdot (0.3)^1$

P U T   T H I S   O N
10,000 9.04 98.01   0.027 512 43.56 729   144 0.0001

M Y   B I L L !
343 128   625 4.41 1 1,024

Page 2

Page 3

Scientific Notation
Skill: scientific notation

Name _____

In what area of the world is it against the law to show or make films that contain kissing scenes?

To find out, find the following numbers written in scientific notation at the bottom of the page and put the corresponding letter above each.

E. 0.00000000361
E. 3,610,000,000,000,000
T. 0.0000000000361
L. 0.0000000000000361
N. 3,610,000,000,000,000,000
A. 0.00000000000000361
W. 3,610,000,000,000

D. 36,100,000,000
A. 0.00000000000361
I. 361,000,000,000
S. 0.0000000000000000361
N. 36,100,000,000,000
B. 36,100,000,000,000,000,000
I. 0.0000000000000000000361

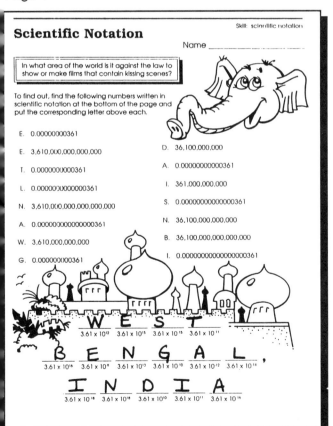

W E S T
3.61×10^{12} 3.61×10^{15} 3.61×10^{15} 3.61×10^{11}

B E N G A L ,
3.61×10^{16} 3.61×10^9 3.61×10^{13} 3.61×10^{10} 3.61×10^{12} 3.61×10^{14}

I N D I A
3.61×10^{18} 3.61×10^{16} 3.61×10^{10} 3.61×10^{11} 3.61×10^{16}

Page 3

Page 4

Primes and Composites
Skill: prime and composite numbers

Name _____

Complete the table.

	Number	Prime or Composite	Factors
1.	56	C	2,28,4,14,7,8
2.	64	C	2,32,4,16,8
3.	97	P	
4.	18	C	2,9,3,6
5.	45	C	3,15,5,9
6.	22	C	2,11
7.	59	P	
8.	8	C	2,4
9.	41	P	
10.	98	C	2,49,7,14
11.	70	C	2,35,5,14,7,10
12.	63	C	3,21,7,9
13.	17	P	
14.	120	C	2,60,3,40,4,30,5,24, 6,20,8,15,10,12
15.	61	P	
16.	33	C	3,11
17.	78	C	2,39,3,26,6,13
18.	103	P	
19.	84	C	2,42,3,28,4,21,6,14, 7,12
20.	29	P	

Page 4

Prime Factorization

Skill: prime factorization

Name _____

Draw lines from the composite number to its prime factorization and then to the prime factorization written in exponential notation.

Composite Number	Prime Factorization	Exponential Notation
1. 96	72 $2 \times 2 \times 2 \times 3 \times 3$	396 $2^2 \times 3^2 \times 11$
2. 52	1,020 $2 \times 2 \times 3 \times 5 \times 17$	320 $2^6 \times 5$
3. 85	189 $3 \times 3 \times 3 \times 7$	56 $2^3 \times 7$
4. 315	686 $2 \times 7 \times 7 \times 7$	52 $2^2 \times 13$
5. 171	96 $2 \times 2 \times 2 \times 2 \times 2 \times 3$	315 $3^2 \times 5 \times 7$
6. 184	162 $2 \times 3 \times 3 \times 3 \times 3$	336 $2^4 \times 3 \times 7$
7. 945	320 $2 \times 2 \times 2 \times 2 \times 2 \times 2 \times 5$	85 5×17
8. 198	315 $3 \times 3 \times 5 \times 7$	171 $3^2 \times 19$
9. 686	256 $2 \times 2 \times 2 \times 2 \times 2 \times 2 \times 2 \times 2$	72 $2^3 \times 3^2$
10. 90	945 $3 \times 3 \times 3 \times 5 \times 7$	126 $2 \times 3^2 \times 7$
11. 126	396 $2 \times 2 \times 3 \times 3 \times 11$	1,020 $2^2 \times 3 \times 5 \times 17$
12. 72	198 $2 \times 3 \times 3 \times 11$	189 $3^3 \times 7$
13. 396	184 $2 \times 2 \times 2 \times 23$	686 2×7^3
14. 1,020	85 5×17	90 $2 \times 3^2 \times 5$
15. 256	336 $2 \times 2 \times 2 \times 2 \times 3 \times 7$	184 $2^3 \times 23$
16. 189	56 $2 \times 2 \times 2 \times 7$	96 $2^5 \times 3$
17. 162	171 $3 \times 3 \times 19$	256 2^8
18. 56	52 $2 \times 2 \times 13$	198 $2 \times 3^2 \times 11$
19. 320	126 $2 \times 3 \times 3 \times 7$	945 $3^3 \times 5 \times 7$
20. 336	90 $2 \times 3 \times 3 \times 5$	162 2×3^4

GCF

Skill: greatest common factor

Name _____

What was John Wayne's real name?

Find the greatest common factor to the following pairs of numbers at the bottom of the page and put the corresponding letter above each to get the answer.

A. 16, 80	O. 55, 88	A. 25, 30	S. 52. 48
I. 70, 42	I. 92, 69	O. 30, 75	R. 18. 45
H. 26, 65	N. 24, 36	M. 27, 12	C. 34, 85
I. 66, 42	N. 110, 42	L. 99, 132	R. 21, 49
O. 125, 75	E. 76, 34	R. 36, 63	M. 88, 48
M. 63, 84			

M A R I O N
3 5 7 23 11 10

M I C H A E L
8 14 17 13 16 2 33

M O R R I S O N
21 15 9 18 6 4 25 12

LCM

Skill: least common multiple

Name _____

Draw lines from the pair of numbers in the doughnuts to their least common multiple in the coffee mugs.

Absolute Value

Skill: absolute value

Name _____

Who is Quasimodo?

Find the integers at the bottom of the page and put the corresponding letter above each to spell out the answer to this question.

H. $|18|$	T. $|-46 + 29|$	H. $|32 - 38|$	M. $|-14 - 13|$
E. $|-12| - 17$	K. $|20 + -25|$	N. $|-15|$	E. $|2 - 16|$
O. $|13 + -9|$	A. $|-12|$	O. $8 - |-17|$	C. $|-20 - 2|$
E. $|-7| - |13|$	F. $|-26| - 40$	D. $|2 + -5|$	C. $|11| - |-42|$
T. $1 - |19|$	H. $|9|$	N. $|17 - 33|$	C. $|8 - 16|$
R. $|-5 - 19|$	U. $|-38 + 5|$		
A. $1 - |-17|$			

T H E   H U N C H B A C K
-18 6 -6   9 33 15 22 18 8 12 -31 5

O F   N O T R E   D A M E
4 -14   16 -9 17 24 -5   3 -16 27 14

ANSWER KEY

Order of Operations
Skill: order of operations

Name _____

Put the following in increasing order.

- [3] $(20 + 5 \cdot 8 + 2 \times 4) + (25 - 16 + 11 - 7 + 3)$ **4**
- [9] $(42 + 18 - 54) \times \sqrt{100} + (9^2 - 11 \times 6) \times (36 - 34 + 1^4)$ **12**
- [2] $(26 - 5^2 + \sqrt{16}) \times (70 + 7 + 4 - 2^3) + (4^2 - 6)$ **3**
- [10] $8 \times 6 + 33 + 11 - 7 \times 6 + 6^2 \div 2 - 63 + 9 \times 2$ **13**
- [8] $92 - (48 + 8 \times 5 \div 3 - 2)^2 + 16 + 4 \times 5 + 2 \times 7 - 4 \times (20 + \sqrt{4})$ **10**
- [12] $77 + (7 \times 8 - 5 \times 9) \times 4 - 48 + 2^2$ **16**
- [4] $(20 - 9 + 28 - 17 + 7 - 24)^2 + (99 + 33 + \sqrt[3]{8})$ **5**
- [5] $(4^2 - 3^2) \times (\sqrt{36} + \sqrt{144}) + (5^2 - 2^2)$ **6**
- [7] $(8 \times 3 - 5 \times 4 + 6^2 - 1^7 + 11 \times 2 + \sqrt[3]{8}) + \sqrt{49}$ **9**
- [11] $(5 \times 12 + 10 \times 7 + 31 \times 3) + (88 + 11 \times 3 - 75 + 5)$ **15**
- [6] $(64 - 11 \times 3 + 52 + 4 - 72 + 8 + 3 \times 7) + (13 - 4 + 5 - 7)$ **8**
- [1] $84 + (5^2 + 4 - 15) + 6 \times (\sqrt[4]{16}) + 3 \times 2 - 48 + (11 + 15 - 23) - 72 + (2^2 + 2^3)$ **2**

Page 9

Fractions
Skill: reducing to lowest terms

Name _____

| What are wine glasses? |

To find out, reduce each of the following fractions to lowest terms and put the letter representing it above the answer at the bottom of the page.

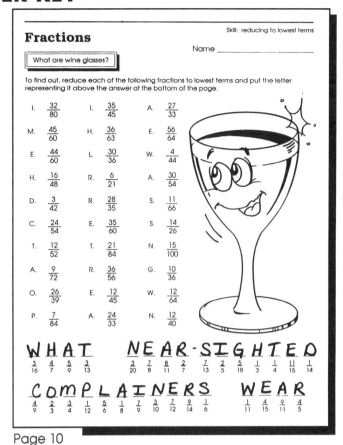

I. $\frac{32}{80}$	I. $\frac{35}{45}$	A. $\frac{27}{33}$
M. $\frac{45}{60}$	H. $\frac{36}{63}$	E. $\frac{56}{64}$
E. $\frac{44}{60}$	L. $\frac{30}{36}$	W. $\frac{4}{44}$
H. $\frac{16}{48}$	R. $\frac{6}{21}$	A. $\frac{30}{54}$
D. $\frac{3}{42}$	R. $\frac{28}{35}$	S. $\frac{11}{66}$
C. $\frac{24}{54}$	E. $\frac{35}{60}$	S. $\frac{14}{26}$
T. $\frac{12}{52}$	T. $\frac{21}{84}$	N. $\frac{15}{100}$
A. $\frac{9}{72}$	R. $\frac{36}{56}$	G. $\frac{10}{36}$
O. $\frac{26}{39}$	E. $\frac{12}{45}$	W. $\frac{12}{64}$
P. $\frac{7}{84}$	A. $\frac{24}{33}$	N. $\frac{12}{40}$

W H A T   N E A R - S I G H T E D
$\frac{3}{16}$ $\frac{4}{7}$ $\frac{5}{9}$ $\frac{3}{13}$ $\frac{3}{20}$ $\frac{7}{8}$ $\frac{8}{11}$ $\frac{2}{7}$ $\frac{7}{13}$ $\frac{2}{5}$ $\frac{5}{18}$ $\frac{1}{3}$ $\frac{1}{4}$ $\frac{11}{15}$ $\frac{1}{14}$

C O M P L A I N E R S   W E A R
$\frac{4}{9}$ $\frac{2}{3}$ $\frac{3}{4}$ $\frac{1}{12}$ $\frac{5}{6}$ $\frac{1}{8}$ $\frac{7}{9}$ $\frac{3}{10}$ $\frac{7}{12}$ $\frac{9}{14}$ $\frac{1}{6}$ $\frac{1}{11}$ $\frac{4}{15}$ $\frac{9}{11}$ $\frac{4}{5}$

Page 10

Fractions as Percents
Skill: writing fractions as percents

Name _____

| What musical group can open any safe? |

To find out, write the following fractions as percents and put the letters above the answers at the bottom of the page.

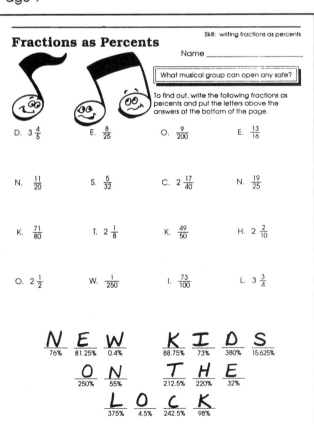

D. $3\frac{4}{5}$ E. $\frac{8}{25}$ O. $\frac{9}{200}$ E. $\frac{13}{16}$

N. $\frac{11}{20}$ S. $\frac{5}{32}$ C. $2\frac{17}{40}$ N. $\frac{19}{25}$

K. $\frac{71}{80}$ T. $2\frac{1}{8}$ K. $\frac{49}{50}$ H. $2\frac{2}{10}$

O. $2\frac{1}{2}$ W. $\frac{1}{250}$ I. $\frac{73}{100}$ L. $3\frac{3}{4}$

N E W   K I D S
76% 81.25% 0.4%   88.75% 73% 380% 15.625%

O N   T H E
250% 55%   212.5% 220% 32%

L O C K
375% 4.5% 242.5% 98%

Page 11

Decimals as Percents
Skill: writing decimals as percents

Name _____

Circle the letters representing decimals that have been correctly written as percents. Read these from top to bottom to finish the following sentence:

| There is an odd law in New Jersey concerning food. This law makes it illegal to: |

- T. 2.34 = 23.4%
- (S.) 4.8 = 480%
- A. 0.0005 = 0.5%
- M. 0.63 = 6.3%
- (L.) 0.0006 = 0.06%
- R. 0.47 = 4.7%
- O. 3.04 = 30.04%
- (U.) 0.0495 = 4.95%
- N. 2.994 = 29.94%
- (R.) 6.0 = 600%
- D. 8.088 = 80.88%
- (P.) 0.875 = 87.5%
- C. 0.62 = 620%
- K. 0.05 = 50%

- B. 0.073 = 73%
- A. 0.153 = 153%
- (S.) 3.4 = 340%
- T. 20.1 = 201%
- H. 1.39 = 13.9%
- (O.) 0.099 = 9.9%
- R. 0.0004 = 0.4%
- (U.) 1.111 = 111.1%
- S. 6.006 = 600.06%
- E. 0.0112 = 11.2%
- (P.) 0.0025 = 0.25%
- I. 7.4 = 74%
- C. 0.8256 = 8.256%
- Y. 9.09 = 90.9%

Page 12

ANSWER KEY

Fractions, Decimals and Percents

Name _____

Complete the table.

	Fraction	Decimal	Percent
1.	$\frac{7}{8}$	0.875	87.5%
2.	19/20	0.95	95%
3.	1/125	0.008	0.8%
4.	3/250	0.012	1.2%
5.	$\frac{19}{40}$	0.475	4.75%
6.	6 33/50	6.66	666%
7.	91/200	0.455	45.5%
8.	19/50	0.38	38%
9.	$\frac{17}{25}$	0.68	68%
10.	21/1000	0.021	2.1%
11.	3/16	0.1875	18.75%
12.	$5\frac{4}{5}$	5.8	580%
13.	9/20	0.45	45%
14.	1/32	0.03125	3.125%
15.	99/100	0.99	99%
16.	$8\frac{3}{100}$	8.03	803%

Page 13

Rational and Irrational Numbers

Name _____

What do you give a piglet with diaper rash?

Circle the letters representing irrational numbers. Read these from the top down to get the answer.

A. 0.063490634906...

D. 618.49875234920006

(O.) 55.06620662066200662...

R. 0.0000000500050005...

F. 0.213699213699213...

(I.) 98.68788898182838485818...

L. 14.68911391139113...

T. 0.004872368777712

(N.) 0.00000000000000987...

A. 8.23538297642898989...

N. 0.438666666666666464646...

R. 23.0000675526755267...

(K.) 4.2388723887238877238...

T. 0.009113041256844424242...

(M.) 6.4444445555686876856...

O. 38.410234556823782828...

I. 555.555555555555685685...

(E.) 9.9985444322227884...

L. 0.64389626438962643896...

R. 29.458895113203203203...

(N.) 1.73085249765100325987...

S. 0.0000007101268446767...

T. 8.0123688924589245892...

M. 1,000.0487231148768934343...

B. 97.04568773456877345...

C. 1.8350016873063333333...

(T.) 0.00438438438143843843243...

E. 0.04896888139688813968...

S. 9.2213344522133445221...

R. 0.00000000000000000068456845...

D. 382.500563400300200200200...

Page 14

Mixed Practice

Name _____

1. Write as a percent.
   1.005   100.5%

2. Is this number rational or (irrational)?
   0.034134413444134...

3. Write the numeral.
   8^3 512

4. List all the factors of 90.
   2, 45, 3, 30, 5, 18, 6, 15, 9, 10

5. Write in scientific notation.
   89,600,000,000,000,000
   8.96 x 10^{16}

6. Find the LCM of the pair of numbers.
   25, 6   150

7. Solve.
   $(3^2 + 11) - 4 + 25 + 5 \times \sqrt[3]{8}$ 26

8. Solve.
   -8 + |-20| 12

9. Write in standard form.
   1.41 x 10^{13}
   0.000000000000141

10. Find the GCF of the pair of numbers.
    7   35, 56

11. Write in lowest terms.
    5/12 $\frac{40}{96}$

12. Write as percent.
    93.75% $\frac{15}{16}$

13. Solve.
    $(0.5)^8 + (0.5)^5$
    0.125

14. Write as a decimal and as a fraction.
    32.5%
    0.325 = 13/40

15. Write in lowest terms.
    $\frac{72}{99}$ 8/11

16. Write the prime factorization of 1,980.
    $2^2 \times 3^2 \times 5 \times 11$

Page 15

Metric Units of Length

Name _____

Complete the table.

	kilometer km	hectometer hm	dekameter dam	meter m	decimeter dm	centimeter cm	millimeter mm
1.	0.008	0.08	0.8	8	80	800	8,000
2.	0.032	0.32	3.2	32	320	3,200	32,000
3.	0.067	0.67	6.7	67	670	6,700	67,000
4.	0.095	0.95	9.5	95	950	9,500	95,000
5.	0.00073	0.0073	0.073	0.73	7.3	73	730
6.	0.001	0.01	0.1	1	10	100	1,000
7.	0.0046	0.046	0.46	4.6	46	460	4,600
8.	0.02	0.2	2	20	200	2,000	20,000
9.	0.00088	0.0088	0.088	0.88	8.8	88	880
10.	3.1	31	310	3,100	31,000	310,000	3,100,000
11.	0.015	0.15	1.5	15	150	1,500	15,000
12.	0.000009	0.00009	0.0009	0.009	0.09	0.9	9
13.	0.000005	0.00005	0.0005	0.005	0.05	0.5	5
14.	7	70	700	7,000	70,000	700,000	7,000,000
15.	0.00043	0.0043	0.043	0.43	4.3	43	430
16.	0.00006	0.0006	0.006	0.06	0.6	6	60

Page 16

ANSWER KEY

Metric Units of Capacity

Name _____

Fill in the missing units.

1. 81 daL = 8,100 __dL__
2. 20 cL = 0.02 __daL__
3. 3.6 L = 0.0036 __kL__
4. 225 dL = 22,500 __mL__
5. 0.05 kL = 5,000 __cL__
6. 18 hL = 1.8 __kL__
7. 28 mL = 0.028 __L__
8. 31,000 mL = 0.031 __kL__
9. 0.4 cL = 4 __mL__
10. 40 L = 400 __dL__
11. 731 dL = 7.31 __daL__
12. 5 daL = 0.5 __hL__
13. 0.009 hL = 9 __dL__
14. 62 L = 6,200 __cL__
15. 1 kL = 100,000 __cL__
16. 1.5 cL = 15 __mL__

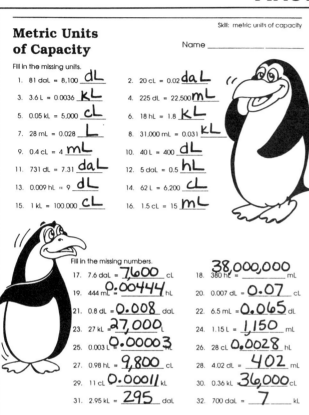

Fill in the missing numbers.

17. 7.6 daL = __7,600__ cL
18. 380 hL = __38,000,000__ mL
19. 444 mL = __0.00444__ hL
20. 0.007 dL = __0.07__ cL
21. 0.8 dL = __0.008__ daL
22. 6.5 mL = __0.065__ dL
23. 27 kL = __27,000__ L
24. 1.15 L = __1,150__ mL
25. 0.003 L = __0.00003__
26. 28 cL = __0.0028__ hL
27. 0.98 hL = __9,800__ cL
28. 4.02 dL = __402__ mL
29. 11 cL = __0.00011__ kL
30. 0.36 kL = __36,000__ cL
31. 2.95 kL = __295__ daL
32. 700 daL = __7__ kL

Metric Units of Weight

Name _____

Complete the table.

	kilogram	hectogram	dekagram	gram	decigram	centigram	milligram
	kg	hg	dag	g	dg	cg	mg
1.	0.005	0.05	0.5	5	50	500	5,000
2.	0.003	0.03	0.3	3	30	300	3,000
3.	0.0085	0.085	0.85	8.5	85	850	8,500
4.	2.5	25	250	2,500	25,000	250,000	2,500,000
5.	0.000602	0.00602	0.0602	0.602	6.02	60.2	602
6.	0.089	0.89	8.9	89	890	8,900	89,000
7.	2.81	28.1	281	2,810	28,100	281,000	2,810,000
8.	0.000012	0.00012	0.0012	0.012	0.12	1.2	12
9.	0.0046	0.046	0.46	4.6	46	460	4,600
10.	0.7	7	70	700	7,000	70,000	700,000
11.	0.03	0.3	3	30	300	3,000	30,000
12.	0.0000715	0.000715	0.00715	0.0715	0.715	7.15	71.5
13.	0.000006	0.00006	0.0006	0.006	0.06	0.6	6
14.	0.04301	0.4301	4.301	43.01	430.1	4,301	43,010
15.	39	390	3,900	39,000	390,000	3,900,000	39,000,000
16.	0.00512	0.0512	0.512	5.12	51.2	512	5,120

Temperature

Name _____

What do you call a duck with fangs?

Find the Celsius temperatures for the following Kelvin temperatures at the bottom of the page and put the corresponding letter above each to solve the riddle.

C. 287.15 K
U. 374.15 K
K. 257.15 K
T. 293.35 K

L. 328.65 K
U. 207 K
O. 269.15 K
A. 228.4 K
A. 393.15 K
C. 302 K
U. 285.15 K
N. 306.9 K
Q. 167.5 K

C O U N T
28.85°C -4°C 101°C 33.75°C 20.2°C

Q U A C K U L A
-105.65°C -66.15°C 120°C 14°C -16°C 12°C 55.5°C -44.75°C

Elapsed Time

Name _____

1. Lethargic Larry left his loft at 1:30 p.m. and arrived at Peppy Pete's place at 6:00 p.m. How long did it take Larry to get there? __4 hr 30 min__

2. Worldly Wanda is flying from San Diego to Las Vegas. She will depart at 6:35 a.m. Pacific time and will arrive at 8:10 a.m. Pacific time. How long is the flight? __1 hr 35 min__

3. Athletic Agnes left her abode at 2:10 p.m. and jogged to Lazy Lucy's lake house. She arrived at 4:55 p.m. How long did it take Agnes? __2 hr 45 min__

4. Bewildered Barry took the bus from Columbia, MO, to Peoria, IL. He departed at 12:11 a.m. Central time and arrived at 6:02 a.m. Central time. How long was the trip? __5 hr 51 min__

5. Convict Carl took the ferry from San Francisco to Alcatraz. The ferry departed at 3:33 p.m. and arrived at 4:17 p.m. How long was the ferry ride? __44 min__

6. Tacky Tom took the train from Stamford, CT, to Manhattan. He departed at 9:53 a.m. and arrived at 10:38 a.m. How long was the ride? __45 min__

7. Sunseeking Sarah is flying from Newark, NJ, to Orlando, FL. She will depart at 10:06 a.m. Eastern time and will arrive at 1:32 p.m. Eastern time. How long is the flight? __3 hr 26 min__

8. Cycling Cyrus rode his bike from Boulder to Colorado Springs. He departed at 11:45 a.m. and arrived at 7:20 p.m. How long did the journey take? __7 hr 35 min__

9. Nell the New Yorker took the subway from Queens to downtown Manhattan. She departed at 5:12 p.m. and arrived at 6:08 p.m. How long was the subway ride? __56 min__

10. Touring Tammy drove from San Diego to San Francisco. She left at 5:40 a.m. Pacific time and arrived at 7:22 p.m. Pacific time. How long was the trip? __13 hr 42 min__

11. Randy the rancher flew from Phoenix, AZ, to Butte, MT. He departed at 11:59 a.m. Mountain time and arrived at 4:06 p.m. Mountain time. How long was the flight? __4 hr 7 min__

12. Patti the politician took the train from Washington, D.C., to Grand Central Terminal in New York City. She departed at 8:32 a.m. Eastern time and arrived at 10:15 a.m. Eastern time. How long was the train ride? __1 hr 43 min__

ANSWER KEY

Mixed Practice

Name _____

1. Write the missing unit.

   73.6 hm = 73,600 __dm__

2. Give the following in degrees Celsius:

   373.05 K

   __99.9°C__

3. Write the missing number.

   515 L = _____ kL

   __0.515__

4. Molly the mountain biker departed at 7:55 a.m. and arrived at her destination at 9:10 a.m. How long did the journey take?

   __1 hr 15 min__

5. Write the missing unit and number.

   58 mL = 0.058 __L__ = __5.8__ cL

6. Give the Kelvin temperature.

   -45°C

   __228.15 K__

7. Write the missing unit and number.

   0.004 kg = _____ cg = 4 _____

   __400__   __g__

8. Flying Freda flew from San Antonio, TX, to Duluth, MN. She departed at 11:25 a.m. Central time and arrived at 4:53 p.m. Central time. How long was her flight?

   __5 hr 28 min__

9. Write the missing number.

   2.5 dg = _____ hg

   __0.0025__

10. Give the Kelvin temperature.

    30 · 85°C

    __304 K__

11. Write the missing number.

    0.0007 mm = _____ dm

    __0.000007__

12. Sightseeing Sara took a bus from Charlotte, NC, to Boston, MA. She departed at 2:37 p.m. Eastern time and arrived at 4:20 p.m. Eastern time the following day. How long was the bus ride?

    __25 hr 43 min__

13. Write the missing number.

    361.9 mg = _____ dag

    __0.03619__

14. Write the missing unit.

    0.26 dL = 0.00026 __hL__

Page 21

Units of Length

Skill: units of length

Name _____

Fill in the missing numbers.

1. 4 ft 9 in. = __57__ in.
2. 3 mi = __5,280__ yd
3. 8 yd 1 ft = __300__ in.
4. 4 yd 21 in. = __165__ in.
5. 6 yd 2 ft = __240__ in.
6. 7 yd 2 ft = __23__ ft
7. 96 in. = __8__ ft
8. 12,320 yd = __7__ mi
9. 324 in. = __9__ yd
10. 54 ft = __18__ yd
11. 8 ft 11 in. = __107__ in.
12. 5 mi = __26,400__ ft
13. 180 in. = __5__ yd
14. 4 yd 1 ft = __13__ ft
15. 4 1/3 yd = __13__ ft

Fill in the missing numbers.

16.
```
   8 yd 2 ft
 - 6 yd 1 ft
```
__2yd 1ft__

17.
```
  10 ft 7 in.
 + 5 ft 7 in.
```
__15ft 14in = 16ft 2in__

18.
```
  11 yd
 - 6 yd 5 in.
```
__4yd 31in = 4yd 2ft 7in__

19.
```
   4 yd 19 in.
 + 1 yd 17 in.
```
__5yd 36in = 6yd__

20.
```
   5 ft 2 in.
 - 3 ft 10 in.
```
__1ft 4in__

21.
```
   7 ft 5 in.
 + 3 ft 9 in.
```
__10ft 14in = 11ft 2in__

22.
```
   6 yd 2 ft
 + 3 yd 2 ft
```
__9yd 4ft = 10yd 1ft__

23.
```
   2 yd 1 ft
 -      11 in.
```
__1yd 26in = 1yd 2ft 2in__

24.
```
  12 yd 1 ft
 - 10 yd 2 ft
```
__1yd 2ft__

25. How many inches are there in 2 yd 9 in.?

    __81 in.__

26. How many yards are there in 36 ft?

    __12yd__

27. How many yards are there in 5 mi?

    __8,800 yd__

28. How many feet are there in 19 yd?

    __57 ft__

29. How many inches are there in 7 1/2 yd?

    __270 in.__

30. How many miles are there in 21,120 ft?

    __4 mi__

Page 22

Units of Area

Skill: units of area

What do you say to a high fashion baby?

Name _____

To find out, find the missing numbers at the bottom of the page and put the corresponding letter above each.

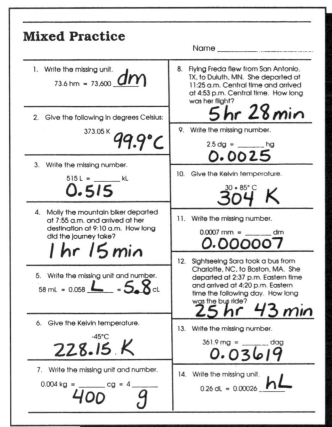

C. 7,040 a = _____ mi²

G. 5 yd² = _____ ft²

I. 3,888 in.² = _____ yd²   O. 3 ft² = _____ in.²

C. 234 ft² = _____ yd²   U. 7 mi² = _____ a   C. 108 ft² = _____ yd²

I. 217,800 ft² = _____ a   G. 2 yd² = _____ in.²   G. 864 in.² = _____ ft²

U. 3 a = _____ ft²   C. 16,848 in.² = _____ yd   O. 11 ft² = _____ in.²

```
  G   U   C   C   I      G   U   C   C   I
  6  4,480 11  13  3     2,592 130,680 26  12  5

          G   O   O
          45  432 1,584
```

Page 23

Units of Volume

Skill: units of volume

What is Shamu's favorite game show?

Name _____

To find out, find the missing numbers at the bottom of the page and put the corresponding letter above each.

N. 243 ft³ = _____ yd³   A. 14 yd³ = _____ ft³

A. 6 ft³ = _____ in.³   H. 139,968 in.³ = _____ yd³

E. 12,096 in.³ = _____ ft³   U. 216 ft³ = _____ yd³

T. 3 1/2 ft³ = _____ in.³   N. 6,912 in.³ = _____ ft³

A. 9 yd³ = _____ ft³   T. 2 yd³ = _____ in.³

M. 7,776 in.³ = _____ ft³   T. 5 ft³ = _____ in.³

```
  N    A    M    E
  4  10,368 4 1/2  7

  T    H    A    T
93,312  3   378  6,048

  T    U    N    A
8,640   8    9   243
```

Page 24

ANSWER KEY

Page 25

Units of Liquid Measure
Skill: units of liquid measure

Name _____

What do you say to your nagging music teacher?

To find out, find the missing numbers at the bottom of the page and put the corresponding letter above each.

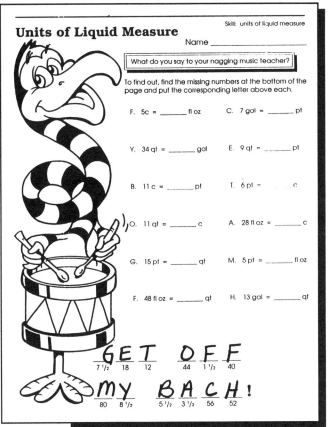

F. 5 c = _____ fl oz

C. 7 gal = _____ pt

Y. 34 qt = _____ gal

E. 9 qt = _____ pt

B. 11 c = _____ pt

T. 6 pt = _____ c

O. 11 qt = _____ c

A. 28 fl oz = _____ c

G. 15 pt = _____ qt

M. 5 pt = _____ fl oz

F. 48 fl oz = _____ qt

H. 13 gal = _____ qt

GET OFF
7 1/2   18   12   44   1 1/2   40

MY BACH!
80   8 1/2   5 1/2   3 1/2   56   52

Page 25

Page 26

Units of Weight
Skill: units of weight

Name _____

In Waterloo, NE, barbers are banned from doing something between 7 a.m. and 7 p.m. What can't they do?

Circle the incorrect inequalities and read these from top to bottom to get the answer about this unusual law.

T. 88 oz = 5 1/2 lb
E. 2 1/2 T = 4,500 lb
L. 8 lb = 128 oz
L. 6,000 lb = 3 T
I. 7 1/4 lb = 116 oz
A. 2 1/4 lb = 44 oz
N. 3/4 T = 1,500 lb
T. 145 oz = 9 lb
G. 112 oz = 7 lb
E. 8 3/4 lb = 140 oz
R. 8,000 lb = 4 T
C. 68 oz = 4 1/4 lb
O. 17 1/2 lb = 284 oz
E. 5 T = 10,000 lb
L. 10 lb = 160 oz
N. 975 lb = 4 3/4 T
E. 64 oz = 4 lb
R. 1 1/2 lb = 24 oz
I. 300 oz = 19 lb
Y. 3 3/4 T = 7,500 lb
O. 9 1/4 T = 18,500 lb
G. 12,000 lb = 6 T
U. 320 oz = 20 lb
N. 7 lb = 120 oz
R. 15 1/4 lb = 244 oz
S. 12 T = 22,000 lb
T. 188 oz = 11 3/4 lb

Page 26

Page 27

Mixed Practice

Name _____

1. How many acres is 6 square miles?
3,840

2. The soda can held 12 fl oz. How many cups is this?
1 1/2

3. How many inches are there in 6 yd 1 ft 8 in.?
236

4. Solve.
4 lb 7 oz
+ 6 lb 11 oz
10 lb 18 oz = 11 lb 2 oz

5. Fill in the missing number.
4 1/4 ft² = _____ in.²
612

6. Fill in the missing number.
5 qt = _____ fl oz
160

7. Fill in the missing number.
9 1/2 ft³ = _____ in.³
16,416

8. Fill in the missing number.
11 ft 8 in. = _____ in.
140

9. How many cubic feet are there in 12 cubic yards?
324

10. How many cups are in 7 gallons?
112

11. Fill in the missing number.
186,624 in.³ = _____ yd³
4

12. Solve.
10 ft 4 in.
– 7 ft 9 in.
2 ft 7 in.

13. How many ounces are in one ton?
32,000

14. How many square feet are in an acre?
43,560

Page 27

Page 28

Angle Measure
Skill: measuring angles

Name _____

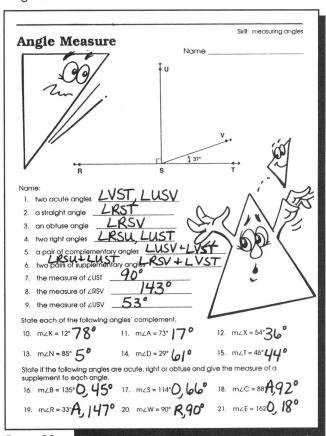

Name:
1. two acute angles **∠VST, ∠USV**
2. a straight angle **∠RST**
3. an obtuse angle **∠RSV**
4. two right angles **∠RSU, ∠UST**
5. a pair of complementary angles **∠USV + ∠VST**
6. two pairs of supplementary angles **∠RSU + ∠UST, ∠RSV + ∠VST**
7. the measure of ∠UST **90°**
8. the measure of ∠RSV **143°**
9. the measure of ∠USV **53°**

State each of the following angles' complement.

10. m∠K = 12° **78°**
11. m∠A = 73° **17°**
12. m∠X = 54° **36°**

13. m∠N = 85° **5°**
14. m∠D = 29° **61°**
15. m∠T = 46° **44°**

State if the following angles are acute, right or obtuse and give the measure of a supplement to each angle.

16. m∠B = 135° **O, 45°**
17. m∠S = 114° **O, 66°**
18. m∠C = 88° **A, 92°**

19. m∠R = 33° **A, 147°**
20. m∠W = 90° **R, 90°**
21. m∠E = 162° **O, 18°**

Page 28

ANSWER KEY

Lines

Skill: parallel lines, perpendicular lines, skew lines and transversals

Name _____

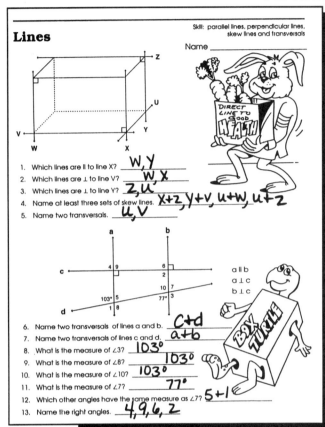

1. Which lines are ‖ to line X? **W,Y**
2. Which lines are ⊥ to line V? **W, X**
3. Which lines are ⊥ to line Y? **Z, U**
4. Name at least three sets of skew lines. **X+Z, Y+V, U+W, U+Z**
5. Name two transversals. **U, V**

6. Name two transversals of lines a and b. **C+d**
7. Name two transversals of lines c and d. **a+b**
8. What is the measure of ∠3? **103°**
9. What is the measure of ∠8? **103°**
10. What is the measure of ∠10? **103°**
11. What is the measure of ∠7? **77°**
12. Which other angles have the same measure as ∠7? **5+1**
13. Name the right angles. **4, 9, 6, 2**

Page 29

Triangles

Skill: scalene, isosceles, equilateral, right, acute and obtuse triangles

Name _____

Name each triangle according to the information given.

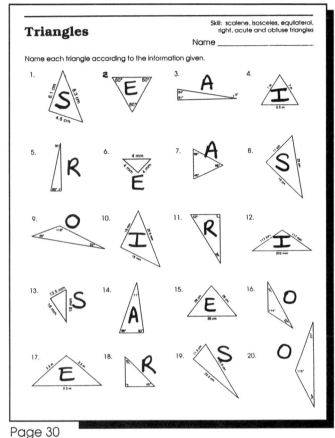

Page 30

Triangles

Skill: finding the measure of the third angle

Name _____

Why did Bart Simpson get suspended from the softball team?

Find the measure of the third angle for each of the triangles at the bottom of the page.
Put the corresponding letter above each correct measure to get the punchline.

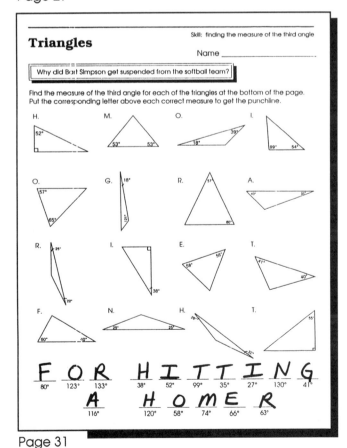

F O R   H I T T I N G
80° 123° 133° 38° 52° 99° 35° 27° 130° 41°

A
116°

H O M E R
120° 58° 74° 66° 63°

Page 31

Polygons

Skill: finding the sum of the measures of the angles

Name _____

Name each polygon and find the sum of the measures of the angles.

1. pentagon **540°**
2. hexagon **720°**
3. heptagon **900°**
4. triangle **180°**
5. decagon **1,440°**
6. octagon **1080°**
7. quadrilaterial **360°**
8. nonagon **1260°**

Page 32

ANSWER KEY

Polygons

Skill: finding the measure of an angle

Name _____

In Omaha, NE, parents can be arrested if their children do what?

To find out, find the degree measure of C in each polygon. Then, find this answer at the bottom of the page and put the corresponding letter above each answer.

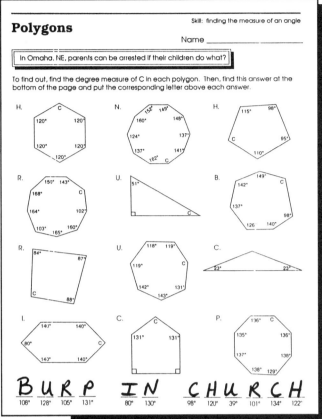

B U R P   I N   C H U R C H
108° 128° 105° 131°   80° 130°   98° 120° 39° 101° 134° 122°

Circles

Skill: parts of a circle

Name _____

Name the following parts of the circle below.

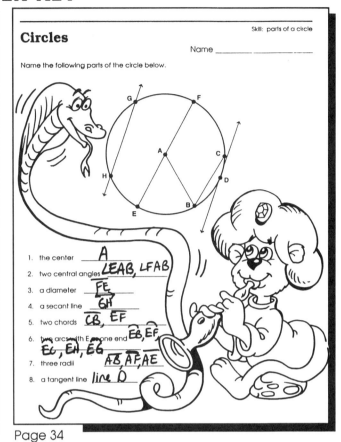

1. the center _____ A
2. two central angles _____ ∠EAB, ∠FAB
3. a diameter _____ FE
4. a secant line _____ GH
5. two chords _____ CB, EF
6. two arcs with E as one end _____ EB, EF
   EG, EH, EG
7. three radii _____ AB, AF, AE
8. a tangent line _____ line D

Construction—Line Segments and Angles

Skill: congruent segments and angles

Name _____

Using a compass and a straight edge, construct a segment congruent to:

Construct an angle congruent to:

Construct the perpendicular bisector of:

Bisect the angles:

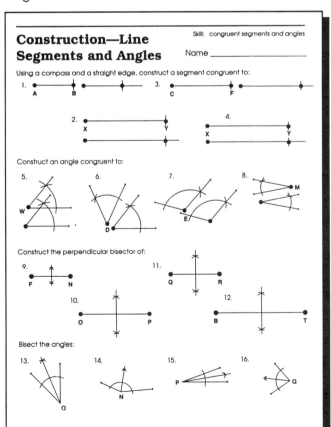

Construction— Congruent Triangles

Skill: side-side-side congruence

Name _____

Using a compass and a straight edge, use SSS congruence to construct triangles congruent to the following:

111

ANSWER KEY

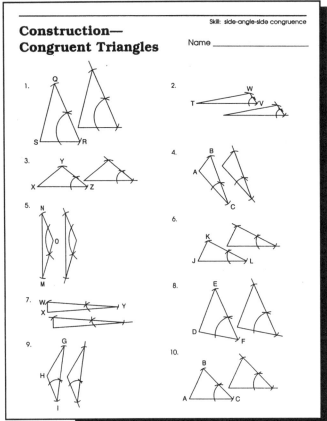

Page 37

Page 38

Congruent Triangles
Skill: SSS, SAS and ASA congruence

Name _____

State if the triangles have SSS, SAS or ASA congruence.

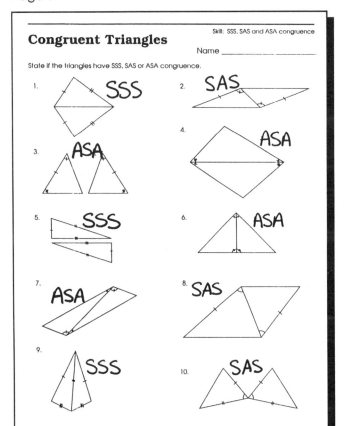

1. SSS
2. SAS
3. ASA
4. ASA
5. SSS
6. ASA
7. ASA
8. SAS
9. SSS
10. SAS

Page 39

Similar Triangles
Skill: similar triangles

Name _____

What do you call a crazy pickle?

To find out, find the length x for each pair of similar triangles. Then, find this answer at the bottom of the page and put the corresponding letter above the answer.

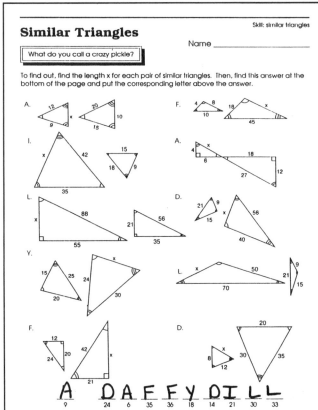

Page 40

ANSWER KEY

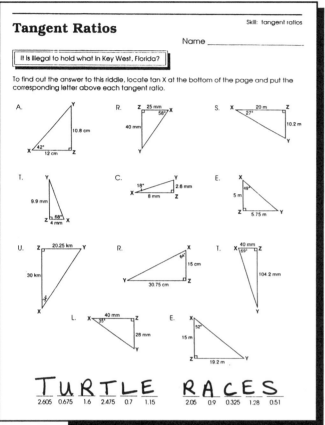

Tangent Ratios

Name _____

It is illegal to hold what in Key West, Florida?

To find out the answer to this riddle, locate tan X at the bottom of the page and put the corresponding letter above each tangent ratio.

T U R T L E   R A C E S
2.605 0.675 1.6 2.475 0.7 1.15   2.05 0.9 0.325 1.28 0.51

Page 41

Table of Tangent Ratios

Name _____

Tangent ratios are rounded to the nearest thousandth.

Angle	Tangent	Angle	Tangent	Angle	Tangent	Angle	Tangent	Angle	Tangent
0°	0.000	20°	0.364	40°	0.839	60°	1.732	80°	5.671
1°	0.018	21°	0.384	41°	0.869	61°	1.804	81°	6.314
2°	0.035	22°	0.404	42°	0.900	62°	1.881	82°	7.115
3°	0.052	23°	0.425	43°	0.933	63°	1.963	83°	8.144
4°	0.070	24°	0.445	44°	0.966	64°	2.050	84°	9.514
5°	0.088	25°	0.466	45°	1.000	65°	2.145	85°	11.430
6°	0.105	26°	0.488	46°	1.036	66°	2.246	86°	14.301
7°	0.123	27°	0.510	47°	1.072	67°	2.356	87°	19.081
8°	0.141	28°	0.532	48°	1.111	68°	2.475	88°	28.636
9°	0.158	29°	0.554	49°	1.150	69°	2.605	89°	57.290
10°	0.176	30°	0.577	50°	1.192	70°	2.748		
11°	0.194	31°	0.601	51°	1.235	71°	2.904		
12°	0.213	32°	0.625	52°	1.280	72°	3.078		
13°	0.231	33°	0.649	53°	1.327	73°	3.271		
14°	0.249	34°	0.675	54°	1.376	74°	3.487		
15°	0.268	35°	0.700	55°	1.428	75°	3.732		
16°	0.287	36°	0.727	56°	1.483	76°	4.011		
17°	0.306	37°	0.754	57°	1.540	77°	4.332		
18°	0.325	38°	0.781	58°	1.600	78°	4.705		
19°	0.344	39°	0.810	59°	1.664	79°	5.145		

Find the degree measure for ∠X.

1. tan X = 0.727 **36°**
2. tan X = 11.430 **85°**
3. tan X = 0.364 **20°**
4. tan X = 0.810 **39°**
5. tan X = 0.194 **11°**
6. tan X = 0.510 **27°**
7. tan X = 1.280 **52°**
8. tan X = 0.425 **23°**
9. tan X = 1.235 **51°**
10. tan X = 19.081 **87°**
11. tan X = 0.158 **9°**
12. tan X = 4.332 **77°**

Find each tangent ratio.

13. tan 70 **2.478**
14. tan 26 **0.488**
15. tan 3 **0.052**
16. tan 82 **7.115**
17. tan 78 **4.705**
18. tan 16 **0.287**
19. tan 49 **1.150**
20. tan 22 **0.404**
21. tan 31 **0.601**
22. tan 53 **1.327**
23. tan 19 **0.344**
24. tan 64 **2.050**

Page 42

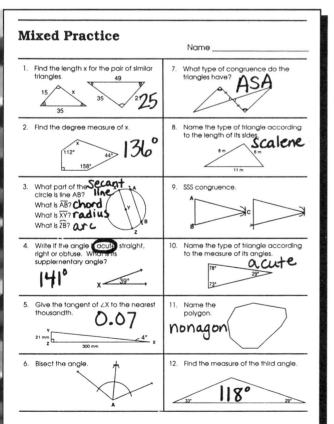

Mixed Practice

Name _____

1. Find the length x for the pair of similar triangles. **25**

2. Find the degree measure of x. **136°**

3. What part of the circle is line AB? **secant line**
What is AB? **chord**
What is XY? **radius**
What is ZB? **arc**

4. Write if the angle is (acute) straight, right or obtuse. What is its supplementary angle? **141°**

5. Give the tangent of ∠X to the nearest thousandth. **0.07**

6. Bisect the angle.

7. What type of congruence do the triangles have? **ASA**

8. Name the type of triangle according to the length of its sides. **scalene**

9. SSS congruence.

10. Name the type of triangle according to the measure of its angles. **acute**

11. Name the polygon. **nonagon**

12. Find the measure of the third angle. **118°**

Page 43

Perimeter

Name _____

Find the sum of the perimeters that make up Paulie the polygon baby.

512 cm

Page 44

ANSWER KEY

Page 45

Area

Skill: area of squares, rectangles and parallelograms

Name _____

What are as unique as fingerprints?

To find out, find the areas of the following shapes. Then, find the answers at the bottom of the page and put the corresponding letter above each answer.

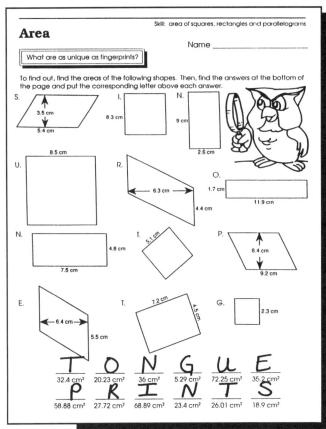

T O N G U E
32.4 cm² 20.23 cm² 36 cm² 5.29 cm² 72.25 cm² 35.2 cm²

P R I N T S
58.88 cm² 27.72 cm² 68.89 cm² 23.4 cm² 26.01 cm² 18.9 cm²

Page 46

Area

Skill: area of squares, rectangles and parallelograms

Name _____

Find the area of each figure.

1. 5.8 cm → **33.64 cm²**
2. 6 m, 10.5 m → **63 m²**
3. 18 cm, 19.8 cm → **356.4 cm²**
4. 8 in, 1 in → **8 in.²**
5. 4.9 m, 2.7 m → **13.23 m²**
6. 22.2 cm → **492.84 cm²**
7. 3.8 m, 11.6 m → **44.08 m²**
8. 14.2 cm → **201.64 cm²**
9. 18 ft, 13 ft → **234 ft²**
10. 2 in → **4 in.²**
11. 16 cm, 3.28 cm → **52.48 cm²**
12. 64 cm, 23 cm → **1472 cm²**
13. 23 ft, 17 ft → **391 ft²**
14. 11.7 m, 8.8 m → **102.96 m²**
15. 29 ft → **841 ft²**
16. 38.5 cm, 42.8 cm → **1647.8 cm²**

17. Square: s = 4.2 cm → **17.64 cm²**
18. Parallelogram: b = 2 ft, h = 3 ft → **6 ft²**
19. Rectangle: l = 8.5 m, w = 6 m → **51 m²**
20. Parallelogram: b = 11 in, h = 18 in. → **198 in.²**
21. Rectangle: l = 6.4 cm, w = 8 cm → **51.2 cm²**
22. Square: s = 53 m → **2809 m²**
23. Parallelogram: b = 23 cm, h = 52 cm → **1196 cm²**
24. Rectangle: l = 4 m, w = 2.7 m → **10.8 m²**

Page 47

Area

Skill: area of triangles and trapezoids

Name _____

Thousands of years after his time, Mr. Geometric Caveman left these cave drawings for you to decode. Find the area of each of the triangles and trapezoids. Then, use the cave drawing decoder box to decipher his message.

Cave Drawing Decoder

A = 808.5 cm²   O = 16.5 cm²   M = 260 cm²
A = 420 cm²   O = 816 cm²   N = 256 cm²
E = 85.5 cm²   D = 115.5 cm²   V = 154 m²
T = 72 cm²   L = 125 cm²   N = 18 cm²

Page 48

Area

Skill: area of triangles and trapezoids

Name _____

Find the area of each figure.

1. 22.3 cm, 56 cm → **624.4 cm²**
2. 11 m, 18.5 m, 4.8 m → **70.8 m²**
3. 7.7 m, 5 m, 13 m → **69.3 m²**
4. 13.2 cm, 4 cm → **26.4 cm²**
5. 25.5 cm, 16 cm → **204 cm²**
6. 6.4 m, 2.1 m, 3.8 m → **36.21 m²**
7. 2.1 m, 11 m, 12.8 m → **81.95 m²**
8. 48 cm, 63 cm → **1512 cm²**
9. 4.4 m, 5 m, 17.4 m → **54.5 m²**
10. 3 in, 18 in → **27 in.²**
11. 112 m, 129.3 m → **7240.8 m²**
12. 9 cm, 11.4 cm, 21 cm → **171 cm²**
13. 16 cm, 15 cm, 28 cm → **330 cm²**
14. 33 m, 104.3 m → **1720.95 m²**
15. 8.2 cm, 27.4 cm → **112.34 cm²**
16. 8.1 cm → **40.095 cm²**

17. Triangle: b = 24 cm, h = 17.7 cm → **212.4 cm²**
18. Trapezoid: b_1 = 4.3 m, b_2 = 11 m, h = 14.9 m → **113.985 m²**
19. Trapezoid: b_1 = 118 ft, b_2 = 126 ft, h = 122 ft → **14,884 ft²**
20. Triangle: b = 5 cm, h = 46.5 cm → **116.25 cm²**
21. Trapezoid: b_1 = 0.8 m, b_2 = 0.5 m, h = 0.6 m → **0.39 m²**
22. Triangle: b = 132 in., h = 56 in. → **3696 in.²**
23. Triangle: b = 14.8 m, h = 19.7 m → **145.78 m²**
24. Trapezoid: b_1 = 10.2 cm, b_2 = 9.6 cm, h = 8.2 cm → **81.18 cm²**

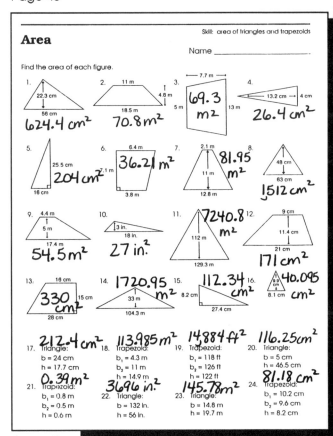

ANSWER KEY

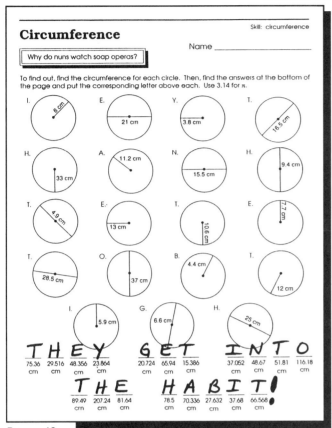

Page 49

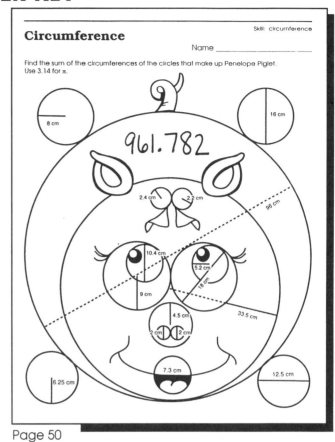

Page 50

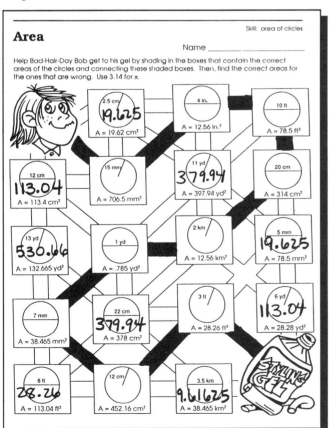

Page 51

Area

Skill: area of circles

Name _____

Find the area of each circle. Use 3.14 for π.

1. (14 mm) $153.86 \, mm^2$
2. (2.4 cm) $18.0864 \, cm^2$
3. (6 m) $113.04 \, m^2$
4. (11 dm) $94.985 \, dm^2$

5. (11 dm) $379.94 \, dm^2$
6. (8.1 m) $206.0154 \, m^2$
7. (18.6 cm) $271.5768 \, cm^2$
8. (39 mm) $1193.985 \, mm^2$

9. (43 m) $5805.86 \, m^2$
10. (1.6 mm) $2.0096 \, mm^2$
11. (114 cm) $10,201.86 \, cm^2$
12. (19.2 m) $1157.5296 \, m^2$

13. (9 m, 12.4 m) $254.34 \, m^2$
14. $482.8064 \, m^2$
15. (22 mm) $379.94 \, mm^2$
16. (100.5 cm) $7928.6963 \, cm^2$

17. r = 16 cm $803.84 \, cm^2$
18. r = 9.9 m $307.7514 \, m^2$
19. d = 25 dm $490.625 \, dm^2$
20. r = 14.1 cm $624.2634 \, cm^2$

21. d = 2.2 mm $3.7994 \, mm^2$
22. d = 158 m $19,596.74 \, m^2$
23. r = 36.7 cm $4229.2346 \, cm^2$
24. r = 88 dm $24,316.16 \, dm^2$

25. r = 100 m $31,400 \, m^2$
26. r = 8.8 mm $60.7904 \, mm^2$
27. d = 5.2 cm $21.2264 \, cm^2$
28. r = 97 mm $29,544.26 \, mm^2$

Page 52

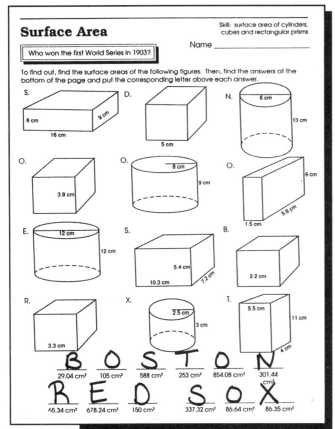

Page 53

Surface Area

Skill: surface area of cylinders, cubes and rectangular prisms

Name _____

Who won the first World Series in 1903?

To find out, find the surface areas of the following figures. Then, find the answers at the bottom of the page and put the corresponding letter above each answer.

S. 6 cm, 9 cm, 16 cm
D. 5 cm
N. 6 cm, 13 cm
O. 3.8 cm
O. 8 cm, 9 cm
O. 6 cm, 1.5 cm, 5.8 cm
E. 12 cm, 12 cm
S. 5.4 cm, 10.3 cm, 7.2 cm
B. 2.2 cm
R. 3.3 cm
X. 2.5 cm, 3 cm
T. 5.5 cm, 11 cm, 4 cm

B O S T O N
29.04 cm²   105 cm²   588 cm²   253 cm²   854.08 cm²   301.44 cm²

R E D   S O X
^5.34 cm²   678.24 cm²   150 cm²   337.32 cm²   86.64 cm²   86.35 cm²

Page 54

Surface Area

Skill: surface area of cylinders, cubes and rectangular prisms

Name _____

Find the surface area of each figure. Use 3.14 for π.

1. 2 cm, 8 cm → **125.6 cm²**
2. 4.3 cm → **110.94 cm²**
3. 4.8 m, 12.5 m, 4.1 m → **261.86 m²**
4. 2.1 mm → **26.46 mm²**
5. 16 cm, 5 cm → **653.12 cm²**
6. 11 m, 16 m, 9 m → **838 m²**
7. 8 m, 2.8 m, 10.5 m → **271.6 m²**
8. 13.2 mm, 1.1 mm, 9.9 mm → **312.18 mm²**
9. 9 cm, 7 cm → **324.99 cm²**
10. 26 m, 7 m, 21 m → **1750 m²**
11. 8 m, 11 m → **502.4 m²**
12. 3.8 m → **86.64 m²**
13. 22 cm, 11.1 cm, 8.1 cm → **1024.62 cm²**
14. 13 m → **1014 m²**
15. 4 cm, 20 cm → **602.88 cm²**

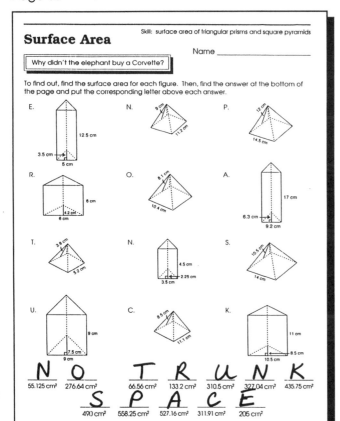

Page 55

Surface Area

Skill: surface area of triangular prisms and square pyramids

Name _____

Why didn't the elephant buy a Corvette?

To find out, find the surface area for each figure. Then, find the answer at the bottom of the page and put the corresponding letter above each answer.

E. 12.5 cm, 3.5 cm, 5 cm
N. 9 cm, 11.2 cm
P. 12 cm, 14.5 cm
R. 6 cm, 4.2 cm, 6 cm
O. 8.1 cm, 10.4 cm
A. 17 cm, 6.3 cm, 9.2 cm
T. 3.8 cm, 5.2 cm
N. 4.5 cm, 2.25 cm, 3.5 cm
S. 10.5 cm, 14 cm
U. 9 cm, 7.5 cm
C. 8.5 cm, 11.1 cm
K. 11 cm, 8.5 cm

N O   T R U N K
55.125 cm²   276.64 cm²   66.56 cm²   133.2 cm²   310.5 cm²   327.04 cm²   435.75 cm²

S P A C E
490 cm²   558.25 cm²   527.16 cm²   311.91 cm²   205 cm²

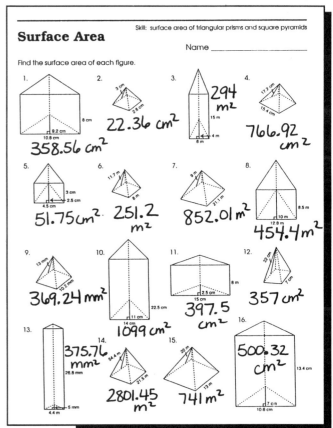

Page 56

Surface Area

Skill: surface area of triangular prisms and square pyramids

Name _____

Find the surface area of each figure.

1. 8 cm, 10.8 cm, 9.2 cm → **358.56 cm²**
2. 3 cm, 2.6 cm → **22.36 cm²**
3. 15 m, 4 m → **294 m²**
4. 17.2 cm, 15.4 cm → **766.92 cm²**
5. 3 cm, 2.5 cm, 4.5 cm → **51.75 cm²**
6. 11.7 m, 8 m → **251.2 m²**
7. 9 m, 21.1 m → **852.01 m²**
8. 8.5 m, 10 m, 12.8 m → **454.4 m²**
9. 13 mm, 10.2 mm → **369.24 mm²**
10. 15 cm, 14 cm, 22.5 cm → **1099 cm²**
11. 2.5 cm, 8 m → **397.5 cm²**
12. 22 cm, 7 cm → **357 cm²**
13. 26.8 m, 4.4 m, 5 m → **375.76 mm²**
14. 54.4 m, 21.5 m → **2801.45 m²**
15. 22 m, 19 m → **741 m²**
16. 7 cm, 10.6 cm, 13.4 cm → **500.32 cm²**

ANSWER KEY

Page 57

Volume
Skill: volume of prisms and cylinders
Name _____

What famous portrait was painted by Humphrey Bogart's mother?

To find out, find the volumes of the following shapes. Then, find the answer at the bottom of the page and put the corresponding letter above each answer. Use 3.14 for π.

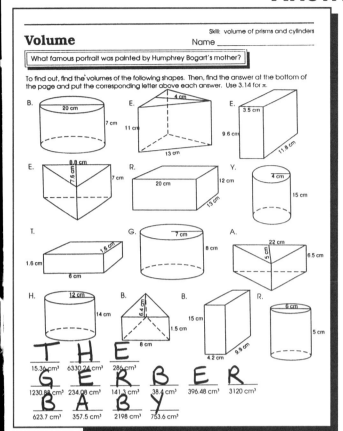

T H E
15.36 cm³ 6330.24 cm³ 286 cm³

G E R B E R
1230.88 cm³ 234.08 cm³ 141.3 cm³ 38.4 cm³ 396.48 cm³ 3120 cm³

B A B Y
623.7 cm³ 357.5 cm³ 2198 cm³ 753.6 cm³

Page 58

Volume
Skill: volume of prisms and cylinders
Name _____

Find the volume of each prism and cylinder. Use 3.14 for π.

1. 549.5 m³
2. 745.2 cm³
3. 697 cm³
4. 345.8 cm³
5. 719.4 m³
6. 1275.2325 m³
7. 18.375 mm³
8. 45.9225 mm³
9. 1749.6 m³
10. 433.5 cm³
11. 5595.48 m³
12. 305.9 cm³
13. 81 cm³
14. 200.96 cm³
15. 27.06 cm³
16. 215.875 m³

17. Triangular prism:
   base area = 7.5 mm²
   h = 9 mm   67.5 mm³
18. Cylinder:
   d = 6 cm
   h = 11 cm   310.86 cm³
19. Rectangular prism:
   l = 4 m
   w = 5.6 m
   h = 7.4 m   165.76 m³
20. Cylinder:
   r = 2.5 mm
   h = 2 mm   39.25 mm³
21. Rectangular prism:
   l = 18.5 m
   w = 16 m
   h = 11.8 m   3492.8 m³
22. Triangular prism:
   base area = 41.2 cm²
   h = 4.5 cm   185.4 cm³
23. Cylinder:
   r = 10 m
   h = 17 m   5338 m³
24. Rectangular prism:
   l = 12.5 cm
   w = 14.5 cm
   h = 4 cm   725 cm³

Page 59

Volume
Skill: volume of pyramids and cones
Name _____

A crazy law in Charleston, South Carolina, requires all horses that pull carriages to do what?

To find out, find the volume of each shape. Then, find the answer at the bottom of the page and put the corresponding letter above each answer. Use 3.14 for π and round to the nearest hundredth.

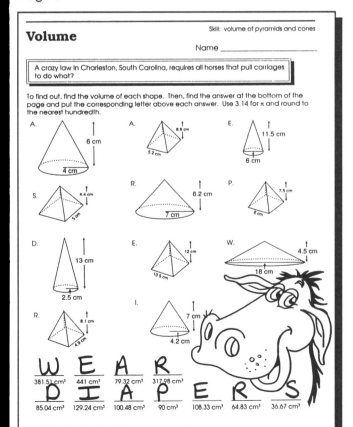

W E A R
381.51 cm³ 441 cm³ 79.32 cm³ 317.98 cm³

D I A P E R S
85.04 cm³ 129.24 cm³ 100.48 cm³ 90 cm³ 108.33 cm³ 64.83 cm³ 36.67 cm³

Page 60

Volume
Skill: volume of pyramids and cones
Name _____

Find the volume of each pyramid and cone. Use 3.14 for π and round to the nearest hundredth.

1. 234.9 cm³
2. 622.98 m³
3. 48.57 cm³
4. 284.96 cm³
5. 53.33 m³
6. 40.02 cm³
7. 58.13 m³
8. 150.27 cm³
9. 293.07 cm³
10. 361.1 m³
11. 326.7 cm³
12. 216.75 cm³

13. Pyramid:
   area of base = 98 m
   h = 11 m   359.33 m³
14. Cone:
   d = 12 m
   h = 10.5 m   395.64 m³
15. Cone:
   r = 5.5 cm
   h = 6 cm   189.97 cm³
16. Cone:
   r = 3.4 cm
   h = 8.1 cm   98.01 cm³
17. Pyramid:
   area of base = 27.5 mm
   h = 7 mm   64.17 mm³
18. Pyramid:
   area of base = 42.25 cm
   h = 9.8 cm   138.02 cm³

ANSWER KEY

Capacity

Skill: capacity

Name _____

When one is honored as "Dentist of the Year," what does he/she get?

To find out, find the capacity for each figure. Then, find the answer at the bottom of the page and put the corresponding letter above each answer. Use 3.14 for π and round to the nearest hundredth.

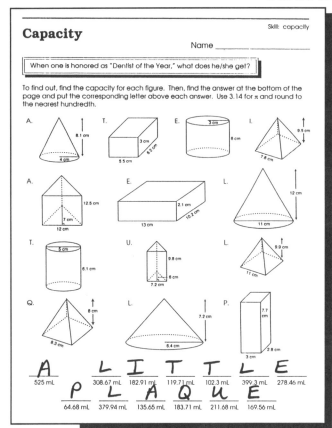

A

525 mL

L I T T L E
308.67 mL 182.91 mL 119.71 mL 102.3 mL 399.3 mL 278.46 mL

P L A Q U E
64.68 mL 379.94 mL 135.65 mL 183.71 mL 211.68 mL 169.56 mL

Page 61

Capacity

Skill: capacity

Name _____

Find the capacity for each figure. Use 3.14 for π and round to the nearest hundredth.

1. 23,314.5 mL
2. 577.5 mL
3. 1102.14 mL
4. 153.6 mL
5. 807.77 mL
6. 117.61 mL
7. 1122.55 mL
8. 440 mL
9. 7182 mL
10. 2711.78 mL
11. 57.38 mL
12. 523.2 mL
13. 22,890.6 mL
14. 475.93 mL
15. (blank)
16. 10,218.96 mL
17. 6860 mL
18. 6916.5 mL
19. 12,911.5 mL
20. 4747.68 mL
(21786.76 mL)

Page 62

Mixed Practice

Name _____

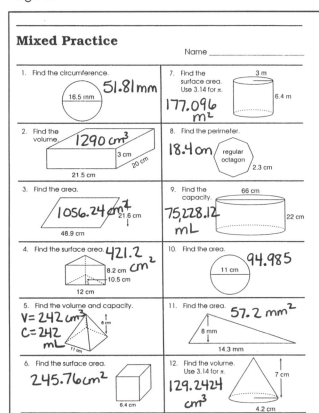

1. Find the circumference. 51.81 mm
2. Find the volume. 1290 cm³
3. Find the area. 1056.24 cm²
4. Find the surface area. 421.2 cm²
5. Find the volume and capacity. V = 242 cm³ C = 242 mL
6. Find the surface area. 245.76 cm²
7. Find the surface area. Use 3.14 for π. 177.096 m²
8. Find the perimeter. 18.4 cm
9. Find the capacity. 75,228.12 mL
10. Find the area. 94.985
11. Find the area. 57.2 mm²
12. Find the volume. Use 3.14 for π. 129.2424 cm³

Page 63

The Basic Counting Principle

Skill: the basic counting principle

Name _____

In Eureka, NV, it is against the law for a man to habitually kiss others if he has what?

To find out, use the basic counting principle to find the answers to the following questions. Find the answers at the bottom of the page and put the corresponding letter above each answer.

GOOD CHOW DINER MENU

H. pizza crust: wheat, white
toppings: pepperoni, onion, mushrooms, sausage, olives, hamburger, green pepper
How many different one-topping pizzas are possible?

U. tortilla: flour, corn, blue corn
fillings: guacamole, bean, beef, chicken, cheese, chili
How many different one-filling burritos are possible?

S. main dishes: hamburger, hot dog, grilled cheese, meat loaf
side dishes: mashed potatoes, cole slaw, French fries, cottage cheese
How many different meals are possible?

M. soups: French onion, clam chowder, chicken noodle, split pea, vegetable
salads: house, Caesar, chef, cobb, pasta
How many different soup and salad combinations are possible?

A. bread: rye, wheat, white, French, sourdough, pumpernickel
fillings: corned beef, ham, chicken salad, roast beef, salami
How many different sandwiches are possible?

A. pasta: penne, angel hair, linguini, gnochi, shells
sauce: marinara, alfredo, clam sauce
How many different pasta and sauce combinations are possible?

C. bagels: egg, plain, onion, garlic
cream cheese: plain, vegetable, pineapple, chive, strawberry, lox
How many different bagel and cream cheese combinations are possible?

E. omelettes: Californian, Western, Spanish, Cheese Lover
fruit: grapefruit, canteloupe, bananas, oranges, blueberries
How many different omelette and fruit combinations are possible?

T. yogurt: vanilla, chocolate, strawberry
toppings: M&M's, hot fudge, pineapple, caramel, granola, Oreo cookie, raspberry
How many different yogurt and topping combinations are possible?

A M U S T A C H E
30 25 18 16 21 15 24 14 20

Page 64

Page 65

Permutations

Skill: permutations

Who brings presents to the dentist?

Name _____

Find the answers to the following sentences at the bottom of the page. Put the corresponding letter above each answer to answer the question above.

S. If 5 cars are selected from 8 and arranged side-by-side in a parking lot, how many permutations are possible?

N. How many 3-digit numbers are there using 2, 4, 6, 8 and 9?

O. How many arrangements are possible with the numbers 3, 4, 8, 9, 11 and 13?

A. How many ways can 7 horses finish win, place and show?

L. How many permutations are there of Annabella, Jake, Sophie, Ellie, Cole, Josie and Miles?

A. How many 2-digit numbers are there using 1, 2, 3, 4, 5, 6, 7, 8 and 9?

S. If 3 books are selected from 11 books and stacked on top of each other, how many arrangements are possible?

T. Jill was making out her class schedule and was interested in math, science, home economics, art, English, French, history and drama. Since she can only take 6 classes, how many arrangements are possible?

S. How many permutations are there of jack, queen, king and ace?

F. How many arrangements are possible with the letters A, B, C, D, E, F, G and H?

$$\underset{24}{S}\ \underset{210}{A}\ \underset{60}{N}\ \underset{20,160}{T}\ \underset{72}{A}$$

$$\underset{40,320}{F}\ \underset{5,040}{L}\ \underset{720}{O}\ \underset{6,720}{S}\ \underset{990}{S}$$

Page 66

Permutations

Skill: permutations

Name _____

Answer the following questions.

1. When Larry asked Abby for her phone number, she wasn't sure if she wanted him to have it. So Abby told Larry that the prefix was 975 and that she couldn't quite remember the last digits but that they were 0, 2, 3, 6, 7, 9. How many possible phone numbers had Abby given Larry to try?   **360**

2. Sam had 9 sweaters. If he wore one a day for a week, how many permutations are possible?   **181,440**

3. How many arrangements are possible using 5 of the letters S, B, R, T, A, D, M, U and L?   **15,120**

4. How many ways can 11 runners come in first, second and third?   **990**

5. How many permutations are there of Janie, Justin, Jack, Julie, Joe, Jeff and Joanna?   **5,040**

6. How many 4-digit numbers are there using the numbers 0, 1, 2, 3, 4, 5, 6, 7, 8 and 9?   **5,040**

7. Ellie was making out her class schedule and was interested in Spanish, English, gym, typing, math, biology, social studies and art. How many different arrangements are possible if she can only take 5 classes?   **6,720**

8. How many permutations are there of yellow, green, blue, purple, red and orange?   **720**

9. In how many different orders can the 8 runners finish the marathon if there are no ties?   **40,320**

10. Bettie bought 10 pillows to try on her couch. She only wanted to keep 4 of them. How many different arrangements were possible?   **5,040**

Page 67

Combinations

Skill: combinations

Whose birth name was Leslie Lynch King, Jr?

Name _____

To find out, find the number of combinations of the following. Then, find the answer at the bottom of the page and put the corresponding letter above the answer.

A. 4 cats from a group of 6

N. 5 songs from the top 10

O. 3 shirts from 7 shirts

E. 6 letters from T, B, M, W, L, D, J, A

E. 4 people from a group of 11

I. 2 sack lunches from a group of 13

L. 5 wolves from a pack of 8

D. 8 students from a class of 15

D. 7 sweaters from a stack of 12

R. 3 puppies from a litter of 9

R. 5 teachers from a conference of 13

R. 4 piglets from a barn of 8

E. 15 cars from a lot of 18

F. 5 kittens from a litter of 9

T. 4 doughnuts from a dozen

P. 6 letters from A, B, C, D, E, F, G, H, I, J

D. 11 necklaces from a jewelry box of 16

R. 7 songs from the top 10

S. 3 books from a stack of 6

G. 5 states from 11

$$\underset{210}{P}\ \underset{1,287}{R}\ \underset{330}{E}\ \underset{20}{S}\ \underset{78}{I}\ \underset{6,435}{D}\ \underset{816}{E}\ \underset{252}{N}\ \underset{495}{T}$$

$$\underset{462}{G}\ \underset{28}{E}\ \underset{84}{R}\ \underset{15}{A}\ \underset{56}{L}\ \underset{4,368}{D}\ \underset{70}{R}\ \underset{126}{F}\ \underset{35}{O}\ \underset{120}{R}\ \underset{792}{D}$$

Page 68

Combinations

Skill: combinations

Name _____

Find the number of combinations

1. 6 songs from the top 10   **210**
2. 7 dresses from a rack of 13   **1,716**
3. 9 doughnuts from a dozen   **220**
4. 5 puppies from a litter of 15   **3003**
5. 6 states from 9 states   **84**
6. 2 letters from A, B, C, D, E, F, G, H   **28**
7. 3 kittens from a litter of 7   **35**
8. 11 cars from a lot of 20   **167,960**
9. 6 students from a class of 14   **3003**
10. 8 sweaters from a pile of 11   **165**
11. 10 people from a group of 13   **286**
12. 5 letters from A, B, C, D, E, F, G, H   **56**
13. 14 stores from a mall of 18   **3060**
14. 5 students from a class of 16   **4,368**
15. 4 finalists out of 17 contenders   **2,380**
16. 13 cars from a lot of 17   **2380**
17. 3 colors from red, yellow, blue, green, purple, orange   **20**
18. 9 wolves from a pack of 14   **2002**
19. 7 numbers from 1, 2, 3, 4, 5, 6, 7, 8, 9   **36**
20. 3 songs from the top 10   **120**
21. 16 students from a class of 20   **4845**
22. 7 doughnuts from a dozen   **792**
23. 12 stores from a mall of 25   **5,200,300**
24. 10 dresses from a rack of 16   **8008**
25. 8 songs from the top 10   **45**
26. 11 states from 18   **31,824**
27. 4 doughnuts from a dozen   **495**
28. 7 puppies from a litter of 11   **330**
29. 4 letters from T, U, V, W, X, Y, Z   **35**
30. 8 books from a stack of 15   **6,435**

ANSWER KEY

Pascal's Triangle

Name _____

Finish Pascal's Triangle through row 15.

```
row 0                              1
row 1                            1   1
row 2                          1   2   1
row 3                        1   3   3   1
row 4                      1   4   6   4   1
row 5                    1   5   10  10   5   1
row 6                  1   16  15  20  15   6   1
row 7                1   7   21  35  35  21   7   1
row 8              1   8   28  56  70  56  28   8   1
row 9            1   9   36  84  126 126 84  36   9   1
row 10        1   10  45  120 210 252 210 120 45  10   1
row 11      1   11  55  165 330 462 462 330 165 55  11   1
row 12    1   12  66  220 495 792 924 792 495 220 66  12   1
row 13  1   13  78  286 715 1287 1716 1716 1287 715 286 78  13   1
row 14 1  14  91  364 1001 2002 3003 3432 3003 2002 1001 364 91 14  1
row 15 1 15 105 455 1365 3003 5005 6435 6435 5005 3003 1365 455 105 15 1
```

Use Pascal's Triangle to answer the following questions. Remember to begin at zero when counting across the rows.

1. How many combinations are there of 12 things taken 3 at a time? **220**
2. How many combinations are there of 8 things taken 5 at a time? **56**
3. How many combinations are there of 14 things taken 11 at a time? **364**
4. How many combinations are there of 6 things taken 3 at a time? **20**
5. How many combinations are there of 15 things taken 8 at a time? **6435**
6. How many combinations are there of 9 things taken 6 at a time? **84**
7. How many combinations are there of 11 things taken 5 at a time? **462**

Probability

Name _____

Find the probability for the die.

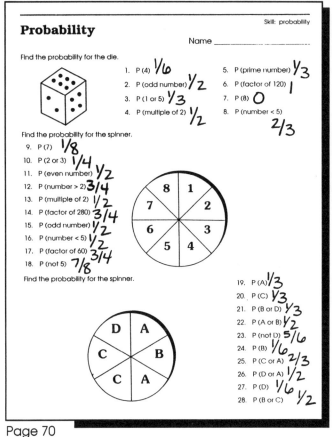

1. P (4) **1/6**
2. P (odd number) **1/2**
3. P (1 or 5) **1/3**
4. P (multiple of 2) **1/2**
5. P (prime number) **1/2**
6. P (factor of 120) **1**
7. P (8) **0**
8. P (number < 5) **2/3**

Find the probability for the spinner.

9. P (7) **1/8**
10. P (2 or 3) **1/4**
11. P (even number) **1/2**
12. P (number > 2) **3/4**
13. P (multiple of 2) **1/2**
14. P (factor of 280) **3/4**
15. P (odd number) **1/2**
16. P (number < 5) **1/2**
17. P (factor of 60) **3/4**
18. P (not 5) **7/8**

Find the probability for the spinner.

19. P (A) **1/3**
20. P (C) **1/3**
21. P (B or D) **1/3**
22. P (A or B) **1/2**
23. P (not D) **5/6**
24. P (B) **1/6**
25. P (C or A) **2/3**
26. P (D or A) **1/2**
27. P (D) **1/6**
28. P (B or C) **1/2**

Probability

Name _____

Think of tossing a penny and rolling a die.

1. How many events are possible? **12**
2. What is P (H, 4)? **1/12**
3. What is P (T, an even number)? **1/4**
4. What is P (T, a factor of 30)? **5/12**
5. What is P (H, number > 3)? **1/4**
6. What is P (T, an odd number)? **1/4**
7. What is P (T, not 4)? **5/12**
8. What is P (H, prime number)? **1/6**
9. What is P (H, 1 or 6)? **1/6**
10. What is P (H, factor of 45)? **1/4**

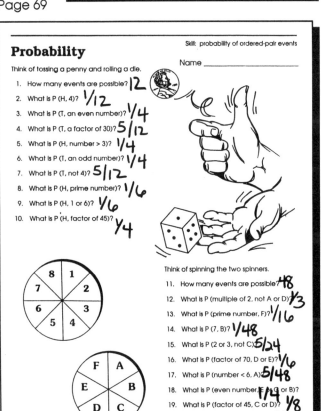

Think of spinning the two spinners.

11. How many events are possible? **48**
12. What is P (multiple of 2, not A or D)? **1/3**
13. What is P (prime number, F)? **1/16**
14. What is P (7, B)? **1/48**
15. What is P (2 or 3, not C)? **5/24**
16. What is P (factor of 70, D or E)? **1/6**
17. What is P (number < 6, A)? **5/48**
18. What is P (even number, F, C, or B)? **1/4**
19. What is P (factor of 45, C or D)? **1/48**
20. What is P (1 or 8, not F or E)? **1/6**

Probability

Name _____

In Durango, CO, it is illegal for people to wear clothing in public places that is what?

To find out, predict the number of times that each event will occur. Then, find the answer at the bottom of the page. Put the corresponding letter above each answer. Round to the nearest whole number.

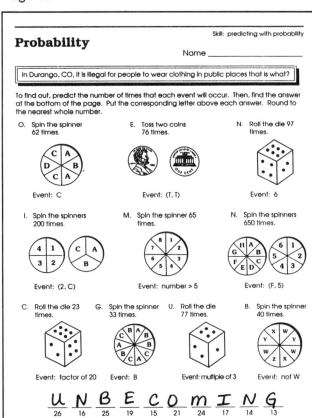

O. Spin the spinner 62 times.
   Event: C

E. Toss two coins 76 times.
   Event: (T, T)

N. Roll the die 97 times.
   Event: 6

I. Spin the spinners 200 times.
   Event: (2, C)

M. Spin the spinner 65 times.
   Event: number > 5

N. Spin the spinners 650 times.
   Event: (F, 5)

C. Roll the die 23 times.
   Event: factor of 20

G. Spin the spinner 33 times.
   Event: B

U. Roll the die 77 times.
   Event: multiple of 3

B. Spin the spinner 40 times.
   Event: not W

$$\underset{26}{U}\ \underset{16}{N}\ \underset{25}{B}\ \underset{19}{E}\ \underset{15}{C}\ \underset{21}{O}\ \underset{24}{M}\ \underset{17}{I}\ \underset{14}{N}\ \underset{13}{G}$$

ANSWER KEY

Odds
Skill: odds

Name _____

Find the odds for each event.

1. Toss both coins.

   Event: both heads $\frac{1}{3}$
   odds in favor = $\frac{1}{3}$
   odds against = $\frac{3}{1}$

2. Without looking, draw a marble from the box.

   Event: drawing a white marble
   odds in favor = $\frac{4}{3}$
   odds against = $\frac{3}{4}$

3. Toss the die.

   Event: factor of 12
   odds in favor = $\frac{5}{1}$
   odds against = $\frac{1}{5}$

4. Spin the spinner.

   Event: getting an A $\frac{3}{5}$
   odds in favor = $\frac{3}{5}$
   odds against = $\frac{5}{3}$

5. Toss the die.

   Event: number < 3 $\frac{1}{2}$
   odds in favor = $\frac{1}{2}$
   odds against = $\frac{2}{1}$

6. Spin the spinners.

   Event: sum of 7 $\frac{1}{7}$
   odds in favor = $\frac{1}{7}$
   odds against = $\frac{7}{1}$

7. Toss the dice.

   Event: sum < 6 $\frac{5}{13}$
   odds in favor = $\frac{5}{13}$
   odds against = $\frac{13}{5}$

8. Spin the spinner.

   Event: even number < 7
   odds in favor = $\frac{3}{2}$
   odds against = $\frac{2}{3}$

9. Toss the dice.

   Event: both numbers the same $\frac{1}{5}$
   odds in favor = $\frac{1}{5}$
   odds against = $\frac{5}{1}$

Probability
Skill: independent and dependent events

Name _____

What is both small and large?

To find out, find the following probabilities. Then, find the answer at the bottom of the page and put the corresponding letter above each.

R. Draw 2 marbles without replacing them.
   P (black, black) = _____
   1st draw 2nd draw

M. Spin each spinner once.
   P (odd number, even number) = _____

M. Toss a die twice.
   P (5, 2) = _____

O. Spin each spinner once.
   P (B, Y) = _____

U. Draw 2 cards without replacing them.
   1 2 3 4 5 6 7
   P (7, 3) = _____
   1st draw 2nd draw

I. Draw 1 marble from each box.
   P (white, white) = _____

H. Draw 2 cards without replacing them.
   1 2 3 4 5 6 7 8 9
   P (# < 4, multiple of 4) = _____
   1st draw 2nd draw

B. Toss a die twice.
   P (# > 4, # > 2) = _____

P. Draw 2 marbles without replacing them.
   P (black, white) = _____
   1st draw 2nd draw

S. Draw 2 cards without replacing them.
   1 2 3 4 5 6
   P (even number, even number) = _____
   1st draw 2nd draw

J. Draw 2 cards without replacing them.
   B A C C A
   P (C, C) = _____
   1st draw 2nd draw

J U M B O   S H R I M P
$\frac{1}{10}$ $\frac{1}{42}$ $\frac{2}{4}$ $\frac{2}{9}$ $\frac{3}{20}$ $\frac{1}{5}$ $\frac{1}{12}$ $\frac{1}{11}$ $\frac{1}{16}$ $\frac{1}{36}$ $\frac{1}{15}$

Mixed Practice

Name _____

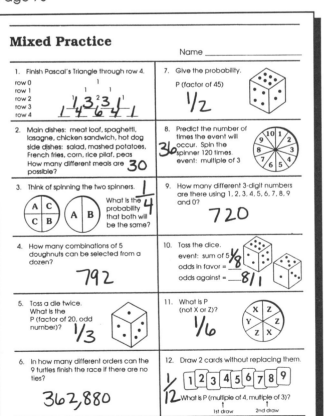

1. Finish Pascal's Triangle through row 4.
   row 0: 1
   row 1: 1 1
   row 2: 1 2 1 → 1 3 3 1
   row 3:
   row 4: 1 4 6 4 1

2. Main dishes: meat loaf, spaghetti, lasagne, chicken sandwich, hot dog
   side dishes: salad, mashed potatoes, French fries, corn, rice pilaf, peas
   How many different meals are possible? **30**

3. Think of spinning the two spinners. What is the probability that both will be the same? $\frac{1}{4}$

4. How many combinations of 5 doughnuts can be selected from a dozen? **792**

5. Toss a die twice. What is the P (factor of 20, odd number)? $\frac{1}{3}$

6. In how many different orders can the 9 turtles finish the race if there are no ties? **362,880**

7. Give the probability. P (factor of 45) $\frac{1}{2}$

8. Predict the number of times the event will occur. Spin the spinner 120 times. event: multiple of 3 **36**

9. How many different 3-digit numbers are there using 1, 2, 3, 4, 5, 6, 7, 8, 9 and 0? **720**

10. Toss the dice. event: sum of 5 $\frac{1}{8}$
    odds in favor = $\frac{1}{8}$
    odds against = $\frac{8}{1}$

11. What is P (not X or Z)? $\frac{1}{6}$

12. Draw 2 cards without replacing them.
    1 2 3 4 5 6 7 8 9
    $\frac{1}{12}$ What is P (multiple of 4, multiple of 3)?
    1st draw 2nd draw

Tables of Data
Skill: tables of data

Name _____

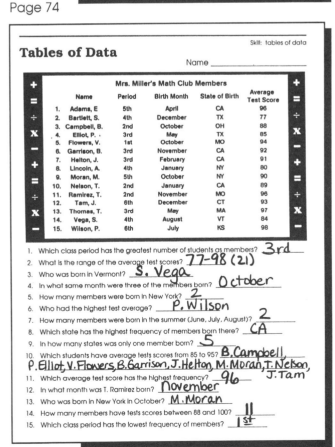

Mrs. Miller's Math Club Members

	Name	Period	Birth Month	State of Birth	Average Test Score
1.	Adams, E	5th	April	CA	96
2.	Bartlett, S.	4th	December	TX	77
3.	Campbell, B.	2nd	October	OH	88
4.	Elliot, P.	3rd	May	TX	85
5.	Flowers, V.	1st	October	MO	94
6.	Garrison, B.	3rd	November	CA	92
7.	Helton, J.	3rd	February	CA	91
8.	Lincoln, A.	4th	January	NY	80
9.	Moran, M.	5th	October	NY	90
10.	Nelson, T.	2nd	January	CA	89
11.	Ramirez, T.	2nd	November	MO	96
12.	Tam, J.	6th	December	CT	93
13.	Thomas, T.	3rd	May	MA	97
14.	Vega, S.	4th	August	VT	84
15.	Wilson, P.	6th	July	KS	98

1. Which class period has the greatest number of students as members? **3rd**
2. What is the range of the average test scores? **77-98 (21)**
3. Who was born in Vermont? **S. Vega**
4. In what same month were three of the members born? **October**
5. How many members were born in New York? **2**
6. Who had the highest test average? **P. Wilson**
7. How many members were born in the summer (June, July, August)? **2**
8. Which state has the highest frequency of members born there? **CA**
9. In how many states was only one member born? **5**
10. Which students have average tests scores from 85 to 95? **B. Campbell, P. Elliot, V. Flowers, B. Garrison, J. Helton, M. Moran, T. Nelson, J. Tam**
11. Which average test score has the highest frequency? **96**
12. In what month was T. Ramirez born? **November**
13. Who was born in New York in October? **M. Moran**
14. How many members have tests scores between 88 and 100? **11**
15. Which class period has the lowest frequency of members? **1st**

ANSWER KEY

Mean, Median and Mode
Skill: mean, median and mode

Name _____

| Where does one go to learn Spanish? |

To find out, use the tables to answer the questions below. Then, put the corresponding letter above the answer at the bottom of the page.

Chuck's Test Scores

math	88
Spanish	73
art	94
science	84
history	73
drama	62

Boxes of Cookies Sold

Amanda	77
Joe	111
Jill	57
Andrew	98
Molly	107
Josh	44
Terry	35
Brad	107
Sarah	66

Birth Months of Students at WJHS

January	89
February	93
March	51
April	64
May	91
June	103
July	46
August	64
September	82
October	123
November	112
December	99

I. What is the median of boxes of cookies sold?

O. What is the mode of Chuck's scores?

E. What is the mean of students born each month?

H. What is the mode of cookies sold?

R. What is the mean of Chuck's test scores?

H. What is the mode of students born each month?

S. What is the median of Chuck's scores?

G. What is the median of students born each month?

N. What is the mean of boxes of cookies sold?

S E N O R H I G H
78.5 84.75 78 73 79   64 77 90 107

Page 77

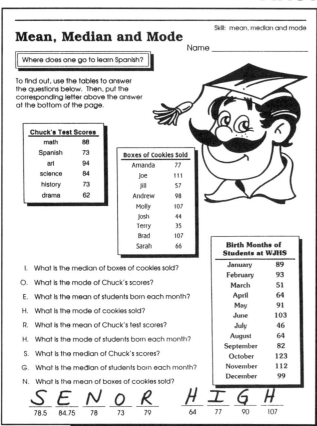

Predicting
Skill: predicting with sample statistics

Name _____

| What do you call 500 rabbits running backwards? |

Favorite Type of Pizza
Sample total: 60 students

Pizza Preferred	# of Students
pepperoni	15
sausage	12
mushroom	6
anchovy	2
Canadian bacon	10
plain	8
other	7

To find out, use the data to answer the following questions. Then, put the corresponding letter above the answer at the bottom of the page.

E. Predict the number of students out of 300 who prefer plain pizza.

E. What fraction of the 50 students buy alternative music?

E. Predict the number of students out of 2,000 who purchase disco.

A. What fraction of the 60 students prefer mushroom pizza?

E. Predict the number of students out of 300 who prefer sausage pizza.

I. Predict the number of students out of 2,000 who purchase jazz music.

A. What fraction of the 60 students prefer anchovy pizza?

I. What fraction of the 50 students buy rock-n-roll music?

D. What fraction of the 60 students prefer Canadian bacon pizza?

H. Predict the number of students out of 2,000 who purchase country and western music.

L. Predict the number of students out of 300 who prefer pepperoni pizza.

N. What fraction of the 60 students prefer a different type of pizza?

R. Predict the number of students out of 2,000 who purchase rap music.

R. What fraction of the 50 students buy blues music?

N. Predict the number of students out of 2,000 who purchase another type of music.

G. Predict the number of students out of 300 who prefer Canadian bacon pizza.

C. What fraction of the 50 students buy classical music?

Type of Music Purchased
Sample total: 50 students

Variety of Music	# of Students
rap	7
rock-n-roll	12
blues	4
jazz	3
classical	1
alternative	10
country & western	2
disco	5
other	6

A R E C E D I N G
1/10 280 60 6/50 40 1/6 120 7/60 50

H A R E L I N E
80 1/30 2/25 1/5 75 6/25 240 200

Page 78

Bar Graphs and Divided Bar Graphs
Skill: bar graphs and divided bar graphs

Name _____

Use the graphs to answer the questions.
1. What type of pizza was purchased most often? _Supreme_
2. How many pizzas were purchased in all? **225 m.**
3. How many more pepperoni pizzas were purchased than plain pizzas? _20 m._
4. 30 million of what type of pizza were sold? **mushroom**
5. How many pepperoni pizzas and sausage pizzas were sold? _80 million_
6. Which type of pizza was purchased the least? _plain_
7. How many other varieties were sold? **40 million**
8. How many supreme pizzas and plain pizzas were sold? _75 million_
9. How many more rock CDs did the 8th graders buy than the 6th graders? _15_
10. Seventh graders purchased the same amount of which two types of music? _alternative + rap_
11. Which type of music did the seventh and eighth graders buy the same amount of? _other_
12. How many rap CDs were purchased by students at Bedrock Middle School? **85**
13. How many more rap CDs did the 8th graders purchase than alternative CDs? _5_
14. Which grade bought 40 rock CDs? **6th**

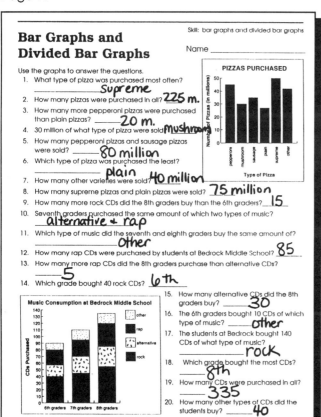

15. How many alternative CDs did the 8th graders buy? _30_
16. The 6th graders bought 10 CDs of which type of music? _other_
17. The students at Bedrock bought 140 CDs of what type of music? _rock_
18. Which grade bought the most CDs? **8th**
19. How many CDs were purchased in all? _335_
20. How many other types of CDs did the students buy? _40_

Page 79

Pictographs
Skill: pictographs

Name _____

Use the graph to answer the questions.

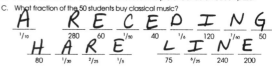

Time Spent Listening to Music

Adults / Teens / Children

Each clock represents 20 million hours.

1. How much time does each clock represent? **20 million hrs.**
2. How many hours do teens spend listening to music? **220 million hrs.**
3. How many more hours do adults listen to music than children? **100 mill. hrs.**
4. Which age group listens to 170 million hours of music? **adults**
5. How many hours do all age groups listen to music combined? **460 mill. hrs.**
6. How many facial tissues does each symbol represent? **50 billion**
7. In which year were 300 billion facial tissues used? **1980**
8. How many facial tissues were used in 1990? **275 billion**
9. How many facial tissues were used in 1980 and 1985? **425 billion**
10. Which two years had the same facial tissue usage? **1965 + 1995**
11. In which year were the largest number of facial tissues used? **1960**
12. In which year were 225 billion facial tissues used? **1970**
13. How many facial tissues were used from 1970 to 1990? **1,125 billion**
14. How many more facial tissues were used in 1990 than 1975? **75 billion**
15. In which year were the fewest number of facial tissues used? **1985**

Number of Facial Tissues Used

1960	
1965	
1970	
1975	
1980	
1985	
1990	
1995	

Each represents 50 billion tissues.

Page 80

ANSWER KEY

Circle Graphs

Name _____

Use the graphs to answer the questions.

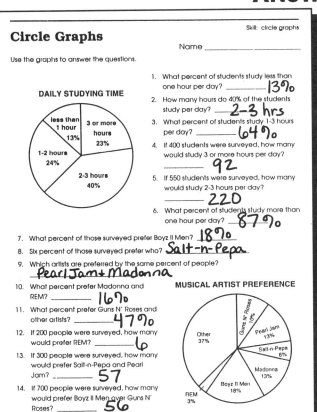

DAILY STUDYING TIME

less than 1 hour 13%
3 or more hours 23%
1-2 hours 24%
2-3 hours 40%

1. What percent of students study less than one hour per day? **13%**
2. How many hours do 40% of the students study per day? **2-3 hrs**
3. What percent of students study 1-3 hours per day? **64%**
4. If 400 students were surveyed, how many would study 3 or more hours per day? **92**
5. If 550 students were surveyed, how many would study 2-3 hours per day? **220**
6. What percent of students study more than one hour per day? **87%**
7. What percent of those surveyed prefer Boyz II Men? **18%**
8. Six percent of those surveyed prefer who? **Salt-n-Pepa**
9. Which artists are preferred by the same percent of people? **Pearl Jam + Madonna**
10. What percent prefer Madonna and REM? **16%**
11. What percent prefer Guns N' Roses and other artists? **47%**
12. If 200 people were surveyed, how many would prefer REM? **6**
13. If 300 people were surveyed, how many would prefer Salt-n-Pepa and Pearl Jam? **57**
14. If 700 people were surveyed, how many would prefer Boyz II Men over Guns N' Roses? **56**

MUSICAL ARTIST PREFERENCE

Guns N' Roses 10%
Pearl Jam 13%
Salt-n-Pepa 6%
Other 37%
Madonna 13%
Boyz II Men 18%
REM 3%

Page 81

Line Graphs

Name _____

CDS PURCHASED AT CITY MIDDLE SCHOOL

(Number of CDs Purchased vs Year, 1988–1995; Males and Females)

1. In 1990, how many CDs did the female students buy? **30**
2. In which year did the male students purchase 40 CDs? **1991**
3. How many CDs did the male students buy in 1993? **65**
4. In which year(s) did the females buy more CDs than the males? **1989**
5. In which year(s) did the male students purchase five more CDs than the female students? **1988, 1990, 1991, 1993**
6. How many more CDs did the male students buy than the female students in 1994? **15**
7. How many CDs did the female students buy between 1990 and 1993? **165**
8. In which year did the female students buy 40 CDs? **1992**
9. How many fewer CDs did the female students buy than the male students in 1990? **5**
10. How many did the males and female students purchase in 1995? **220**
11. How many fewer CDs did the male students buy in 1991 than in 1995? **75**
12. In which year did the students buy 135 CDs? **1993**
13. How many CDs did the students at City Middle School purchase in 1991? **75**
14. How many more CDs did the females buy in 1993 than in 1989? **45**
15. In which year did the students buy 185 CDs? **1994**
16. What is the difference in the total number of CDs purchased by students in 1989 and 1990? **25**

Page 82

Scattergrams

Name _____

State if the following scattergrams show a positive correlation, negative correlation or no correlation.

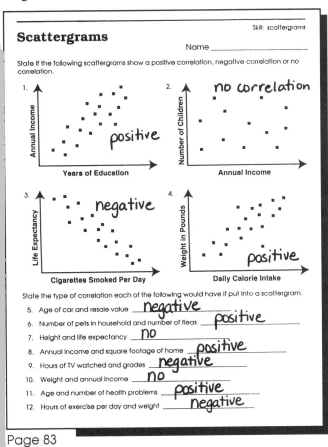

1. Annual Income vs Years of Education — **positive**
2. Number of Children vs Annual Income — **no correlation**
3. Life Expectancy vs Cigarettes Smoked Per Day — **negative**
4. Weight in Pounds vs Daily Calorie Intake — **positive**

State the type of correlation each of the following would have if put into a scattergram.

5. Age of car and resale value **negative**
6. Number of pets in household and number of fleas **positive**
7. Height and life expectancy **no**
8. Annual income and square footage of home **positive**
9. Hours of TV watched and grades **negative**
10. Weight and annual income **no**
11. Age and number of health problems **positive**
12. Hours of exercise per day and weight **negative**

Page 83

Stem and Leaf Plots

Name _____

The weights of all of the babies born at Infantville Hospital on January 13th, 1995 were recorded in ounces as follows: 101, 128, 112, 105, 96, 88, 132, 139, 97, 115, 105, 147, 138, 96, 122, 133, 107, 122, 129, 111, 119, 122, 136, 148, 125, 139 and 124.

1. Put the data in the stem and leaf plot.

Stem	Leaf
8	8
9	6,6,7
10	1,5,5,7
11	1,2,5,9
12	2,2,2,4,5,8,9
13	2,3,6,8,9,9
14	7,8

2. Use the stem and leaf plot to name the value repeated three times. **122**
3. Which three values are repeated twice? **96, 105, 139**
4. Were most babies born below or above 120 ounces? **above**
5. Are there more values with a stem of 12 or a stem of 13? **12**
6. Which stem has three values? **9**

The ages of all the guests at Ellie's 40th Birthday Bash were recorded as follows: 52, 41, 26, 38, 40, 62, 55, 43, 48, 57, 39, 37, 45, 70, 56, 64, 29, 50, 61, 73, 28, 44, 53, 41, 55, 67, 42, 36, 26, 35, 40, 53, 63, 26 and 41.

7. Put the data in the stem and leaf plot.

Stem	Leaf
2	6,6,6,8,9
3	5,6,7,8,9
4	0,0,1,1,1,2,3,4,5,8
5	0,2,3,3,5,5,6,7
6	1,2,3,4,7
7	0,3

8. How many leaves does the stem 5 have? **8**
9. How many times does the age 64 appear? **once**
10. Which age occurs more frequently, 55 or 26? **26**
11. Which stem has the most values? **4**
12. Which stems have 5 values? **2,3,6**
13. Were most of the guests younger or older than 50? **younger**
14. Which values appear more than once? **26, 40, 41, 53, 55**

Page 84

Frequency Tables and Histograms

Skill: frequency tables and histograms

Name _____

1.

Stem	Leaf
0	99
1	99
2	85
3	33
4	91
5	60
6	18
7	12, 56
8	26, 46, 88
9	21, 56
10	00, 48
11	11, 29, 90
12	65, 92
13	16, 99
14	88
15	16, 20
16	21, 29
17	52, 78
18	14, 78, 99
19	15, 25

2. **Frequency Table**

Grouping Intervals	Frequency
0 - $4.99	5
$5.00 - $9.99	9
$10.00 - $14.99	10
$15.00 - $19.99	11

3. **Histogram for Dinner Sales**

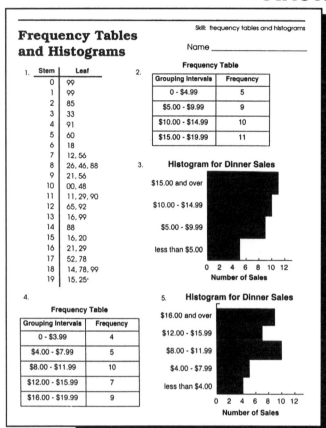

4. **Frequency Table**

Grouping Intervals	Frequency
0 - $3.99	4
$4.00 - $7.99	5
$8.00 - $11.99	10
$12.00 - $15.99	7
$16.00 - $19.99	9

5. **Histogram for Dinner Sales**

Box and Whisker Graphs

Skill: box and whisker graphs

Name _____

Draw box and whisker graphs for the following sets of data. First, make a stem and leaf plot.

1. 96, 52, 38, 66, 72, 81, 87, 65, 48, 91, 75, 82, 49, 56, 78, 65, 90, 71

Stem	Leaf
9	0, 1, 6
8	1, 2, 7
7	1, 2, 5, 8
6	5, 5, 6
5	2, 6
4	8, 9
3	8

H=96, Qu=82, mD=71.5, QL=56, L=38

2. 3.2, 4.1, 3.5, 5.6, 4.2, 2.9, 7.7, 5.4, 6.1, 6.5, 5.8, 4.7, 6.2, 2.8, 4.0, 5.1

Stem	Leaf
7	7
6	1, 2, 5
5	1, 4, 6, 8
4	0, 1, 2, 7
3	2, 5
2	8, 9

H=7.7, Qu=5.8, mD=4.9, QL=4.0, L=2.8

3. 22, 13, 40, 18, 11, 15, 25, 31, 8, 19, 33, 20, 5, 28, 35, 16, 42, 10

Stem	Leaf
4	0, 2
3	1, 3, 5
2	0, 2, 5, 8
1	0, 1, 3, 5, 6, 8, 9
0	5, 8

H=42, Qu=31, mD=19.5, QL=13, L=5

4. 3.3, 2.7, 4.9, 0.6, 1.1, 2.0, 1.5, 3.7, 1.1, 4.2, 4.6, 2.5, 1.7, 3.4

Stem	Leaf
4	2, 6, 9
3	3, 4, 7
2	0, 5, 7
1	1, 1, 5, 7
0	6

H=4.9, Qu=3.7, mD=2.6, QL=1.5, L=0.6

Mixed Practice

Name _____

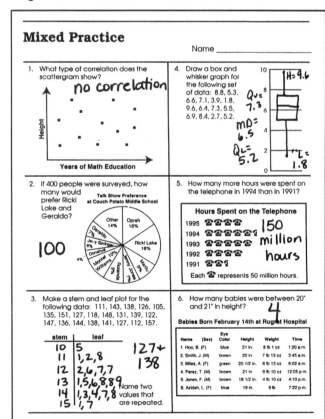

1. What type of correlation does the scattergram show? — no correlation

2. If 400 people were surveyed, how many would prefer Ricki Lake and Geraldo? — 100

3. Make a stem and leaf plot for the following data: 111, 143, 138, 126, 105, 135, 151, 127, 118, 148, 131, 139, 122, 147, 136, 144, 138, 141, 127, 112, 157.

stem	leaf
10	5
11	1, 2, 8
12	2, 6, 7, 7
13	1, 5, 6, 8, 8, 9
14	1, 3, 4, 7, 8
15	1, 7

127 & 138 — Name two values that are repeated.

4. Draw a box and whisker graph for the following set of data: 8.8, 5.3, 6.6, 7.1, 3.9, 1.8, 9.6, 6.4, 7.3, 5.5, 6.9, 8.4, 2.7, 5.2. — H=9.6, Qu=7.3, mD=6.5, QL=5.2, L=1.8

5. How many more hours were spent on the telephone in 1994 than in 1991? — 150 million hours

6. How many babies were between 20" and 21" in height? — 4

Mixed Practice continued

Name _____

7. Predict the number out of 600 students who watched Loving. — 72

8. Make a frequency table with 10-point frequency intervals.

Frequency Table

Grouping Intervals	Frequency	Grouping Intervals	Frequency
0-9	0	50-59	3
10-19	0	60-69	5
20-29	0	70-79	9
30-39	0	80-89	7
40-49	2	90-99	4

9. **Histogram for Scores**

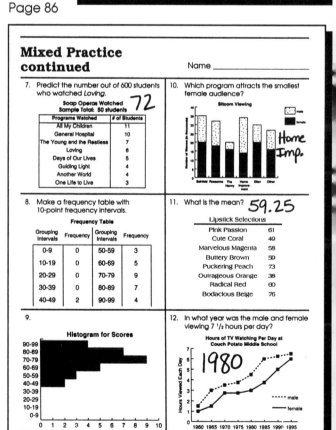

10. Which program attracts the smallest female audience? — Home Imp.

11. What is the mean? — 59.25

12. In what year was the male and female viewing 7 1/2 hours per day? — 1980

Squares and Square Roots

Skill: squares and square roots

Name _____

Did you hear about the student that didn't like school?

To get the punchline, find the square root of each problem. Then, put the corresponding letter above each answer at the bottom of the page.

A. $-\sqrt{81}$ H. $\sqrt{64}$ T. $-\sqrt{36}$ T. $\sqrt{25}$ C. $\sqrt{49}$

N. $-\sqrt{144}$ A. $\sqrt{400}$ R. $\sqrt{121}$ H. $-\sqrt{16}$ F. $-\sqrt{100}$

E. $\sqrt{225}$ I. $-\sqrt{49}$ E. $-\sqrt{196}$ S. $\sqrt{625}$ P. $-\sqrt{1}$

I. $\sqrt{169}$ I. $-\sqrt{9}$ T. $-\sqrt{256}$ W. $\sqrt{36}$ G. $\sqrt{144}$

T. $\sqrt{10,000}$ N. $\sqrt{81}$ H. $\sqrt{100}$ L. $-\sqrt{1,600}$

O. $-\sqrt{900}$ I. $\sqrt{2,500}$ P. $-\sqrt{169}$

$$\underset{13}{I}\ \underset{5}{T}\quad \underset{6}{W}\ \underset{20}{A}\ \underset{25}{S}\quad \underset{-6}{T}\ \underset{10}{H}\ \underset{15}{E}$$

$$\underset{-13}{P}\ \underset{11}{R}\ \underset{-3}{I}\ \underset{9}{N}\ \underset{7}{C}\ \underset{50}{I}\ \underset{-1}{P}\ \underset{-9}{A}\ \underset{-40}{L}$$

$$\underset{-30}{O}\ \underset{-10}{F}\quad \underset{-16}{T}\ \underset{8}{H}\ \underset{-14}{E}\quad \underset{100}{T}\ \underset{-4}{H}\ \underset{-7}{I}\ \underset{-12}{N}\ \underset{12}{G}!$$

Page 89

Square Roots

Skill: finding square roots using a table

Name _____

Tulsa, OK, has an ordinance against what?

To find out, find the square roots of the numbers using the table. Then, put the letter above the square root at the bottom of the page.

Table of Squares and Square Roots

# n	Square n^2	Square Root $\sqrt{n}$	# n	Square n^2	Square Root $\sqrt{n}$
1	1	1.000	21	441	4.583
2	4	1.414	22	484	4.690
3	9	1.732	23	529	4.796
4	16	2.000	24	576	4.899
5	25	2.236	25	625	5.000
6	36	2.449	26	676	5.099
7	49	2.646	27	729	5.196
8	64	2.828	28	784	5.292
9	81	3.000	29	841	5.385
10	100	3.162	30	900	5.477
11	121	3.317	31	961	5.568
12	144	3.464	32	1,024	5.657
13	169	3.606	33	1,089	5.745
14	196	3.742	34	1,156	5.831
15	225	3.873	35	1,225	5.916
16	256	4.000	36	1,296	6.000
17	289	4.123	37	1,369	6.083
18	324	4.243	38	1,444	6.164
19	361	4.359	39	1,521	6.245
20	400	4.472	40	1,600	6.325

A. $\sqrt{34}$ R. $\sqrt{18}$ N. $\sqrt{22}$ S. $\sqrt{2}$

H. $\sqrt{39}$ T. $\sqrt{15}$ A. $\sqrt{5}$ R. $\sqrt{29}$

A. $\sqrt{11}$ H. $\sqrt{28}$ E. $\sqrt{37}$ T. $\sqrt{20}$

T. $\sqrt{8}$ S. $\sqrt{32}$ O. $\sqrt{26}$ R. $\sqrt{33}$

L. $\sqrt{14}$ F. $\sqrt{10}$ H. $\sqrt{19}$ S. $\sqrt{40}$

I. $\sqrt{3}$ S. $\sqrt{1}$ E. $\sqrt{12}$ E. $\sqrt{21}$

I. $\sqrt{13}$ N. $\sqrt{6}$ T. $\sqrt{30}$ M. $\sqrt{7}$

T. $\sqrt{38}$ E. $\sqrt{31}$ O. $\sqrt{27}$ I. $\sqrt{4}$

E. $\sqrt{24}$ K. $\sqrt{17}$ U. $\sqrt{35}$ M. $\sqrt{23}$

S. $\sqrt{36}$

$$\underset{4.123}{K}\ \underset{1.732}{I}\ \underset{6}{S}\ \underset{1.414}{S}\ \underset{4.899}{E}\ \underset{5.657}{S}\quad \underset{6.164}{T}\ \underset{5.292}{H}\ \underset{5.831}{A}\ \underset{5.477}{T}$$

$$\underset{3.742}{L}\ \underset{3.317}{A}\ \underset{1.000}{S}\ \underset{3.873}{T}\quad \underset{3.162}{F}\ \underset{5.196}{O}\ \underset{5.385}{R}\quad \underset{2.646}{M}\ \underset{5.099}{O}\ \underset{4.243}{R}\ \underset{4.583}{E}$$

$$\underset{4.472}{T}\ \underset{4.359}{H}\ \underset{2.236}{A}\ \underset{2.449}{N}\quad \underset{2}{T}\ \underset{6.245}{H}\ \underset{5.745}{R}\ \underset{6.083}{E}\ \underset{3.464}{E}$$

$$\underset{4.796}{M}\ \underset{3.606}{I}\ \underset{4.690}{N}\ \underset{5.916}{U}\ \underset{2.828}{T}\ \underset{5.568}{E}\ \underset{6.325}{S}$$

Page 90

Square Roots

Skill: finding square roots without a table

Name _____

What is another term for beef stew?

To find out, estimate the following square roots to the nearest hundredth using the divide and average method. Then, put the letter above each answer at the bottom of the page. Find the answer closest to your own if one is not exactly the same.

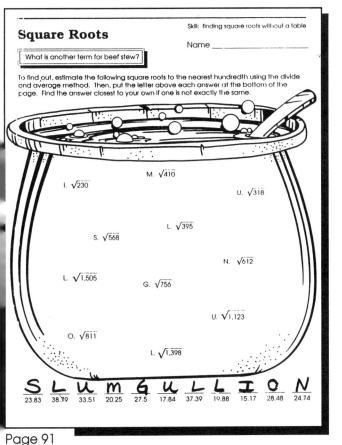

M. $\sqrt{410}$

I. $\sqrt{230}$ U. $\sqrt{318}$

L. $\sqrt{395}$

S. $\sqrt{568}$

N. $\sqrt{612}$

L. $\sqrt{1,505}$ G. $\sqrt{756}$

U. $\sqrt{1,123}$

O. $\sqrt{811}$

L. $\sqrt{1,398}$

$$\underset{23.83}{S}\ \underset{38.79}{L}\ \underset{33.51}{U}\ \underset{20.25}{M}\ \underset{27.5}{G}\ \underset{17.84}{U}\ \underset{37.39}{L}\ \underset{19.88}{L}\ \underset{15.17}{I}\ \underset{28.48}{O}\ \underset{24.74}{N}$$

Page 91

Pythagorean Theorem

Skill: finding the length of the hypotenuse

Name _____

What famous swine created the frescoes on the ceiling of the Pigstine Chapel?

To find out, use a table of square roots or a calculator to find the length of each hypotenuse to the nearest thousandth. Then, put the corresponding letter above each answer at the bottom of the page.

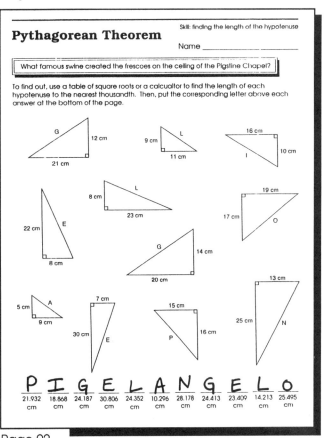

$$\underset{21.932\ cm}{P}\ \underset{18.868\ cm}{I}\ \underset{24.187\ cm}{G}\ \underset{30.806\ cm}{E}\ \underset{24.352\ cm}{L}\ \underset{10.296\ cm}{A}\ \underset{28.178\ cm}{N}\ \underset{24.413\ cm}{G}\ \underset{23.409\ cm}{E}\ \underset{14.213\ cm}{L}\ \underset{25.495\ cm}{O}$$

Page 92

ANSWER KEY

Pythagorean Theorem
Name _____

Skill: finding the lengths of legs of right triangles

What was written on the vegetable farmer's tombstone?

To find the punchline, use a table of square roots or a calculator to find the length of each leg not given to the nearest thousandth. Then, put the corresponding letter above each answer at the bottom of the page.

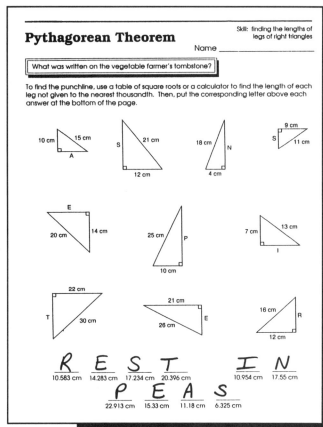

$$
\underset{10.583 \text{ cm}}{R} \quad \underset{14.283 \text{ cm}}{E} \quad \underset{17.234 \text{ cm}}{S} \quad \underset{20.396 \text{ cm}}{T} \qquad \underset{10.954 \text{ cm}}{I} \quad \underset{17.55 \text{ cm}}{N}
$$

$$
\underset{22.913 \text{ cm}}{P} \quad \underset{15.33 \text{ cm}}{E} \quad \underset{11.18 \text{ cm}}{A} \quad \underset{6.325 \text{ cm}}{S}
$$

30°-60° Right Triangles
Name _____

Skill: 30° 60° right triangles

It is against the law to do what when admiring a member of the opposite sex in San Antonio, TX?

To find out, find the lengths of the unknown sides of each triangle using a calculator and rounding to the nearest tenth when necessary. Locate the lengths at the bottom of the page and put the corresponding letter above each.

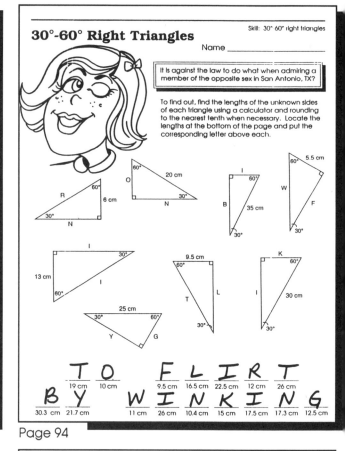

$$
\underset{19 \text{ cm}}{T} \underset{10 \text{ cm}}{O} \qquad \underset{9.5 \text{ cm}}{F} \underset{16.5 \text{ cm}}{L} \underset{22.5 \text{ cm}}{I} \underset{12 \text{ cm}}{R} \underset{26 \text{ cm}}{T}
$$

$$
\underset{30.3 \text{ cm}}{B} \underset{21.7 \text{ cm}}{Y} \qquad \underset{11 \text{ cm}}{W} \underset{26 \text{ cm}}{I} \underset{10.4 \text{ cm}}{N} \underset{15 \text{ cm}}{K} \underset{17.5 \text{ cm}}{I} \underset{17.3 \text{ cm}}{N} \underset{12.5 \text{ cm}}{G}
$$

45°-45° Right Triangles
Name _____

Skill: 45°-45° right triangles

What happened to the girl who stole mascara?

To find out, use a calculator to find the hypotenuse of each triangle to the nearest tenth. Then, put the corresponding letter above each answer at the bottom of the page.

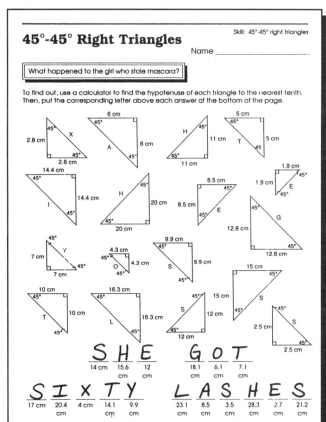

$$
\underset{14 \text{ cm}}{S} \underset{\substack{15.6 \\ \text{cm}}}{H} \underset{\substack{12 \\ \text{cm}}}{E} \qquad \underset{\substack{18.1 \\ \text{cm}}}{G} \underset{\substack{6.1 \\ \text{cm}}}{O} \underset{\substack{7.1 \\ \text{cm}}}{T}
$$

$$
\underset{17 \text{ cm}}{S} \underset{\substack{20.4 \\ \text{cm}}}{I} \underset{4 \text{ cm}}{X} \underset{\substack{14.1 \\ \text{cm}}}{T} \underset{\substack{9.9 \\ \text{cm}}}{Y} \qquad \underset{\substack{23.1 \\ \text{cm}}}{L} \underset{\substack{8.5 \\ \text{cm}}}{A} \underset{\substack{3.5 \\ \text{cm}}}{S} \underset{\substack{28.3 \\ \text{cm}}}{H} \underset{\substack{2.7 \\ \text{cm}}}{E} \underset{\substack{21.2 \\ \text{cm}}}{S}
$$

Sine Ratios
Name _____

Skill: sine ratios

What are galligaskins?

To find out, find sine A to the nearest thousandth and put the corresponding letter above the answer at the bottom of the page.

$$
\underset{0.406}{L} \underset{0.351}{O} \underset{0.554}{O} \underset{0.394}{S} \underset{0.371}{E}
$$

$$
\underset{0.64}{T} \underset{0.625}{R} \underset{0.515}{O} \underset{0.385}{U} \underset{0.446}{S} \underset{0.6}{E} \underset{0.496}{R} \underset{0.316}{S}
$$

ANSWER KEY

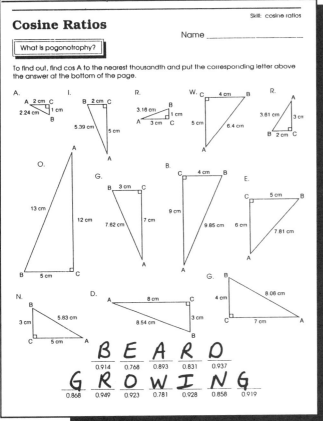

Cosine Ratios

Skill: cosine ratios

Name _____

What is pogonotrophy?

To find out, find cos A to the nearest thousandth and put the corresponding letter above the answer at the bottom of the page.

B E A R D
0.914 0.768 0.893 0.831 0.937

G R O W I N G
0.868 0.949 0.923 0.781 0.928 0.858 0.919

Page 97

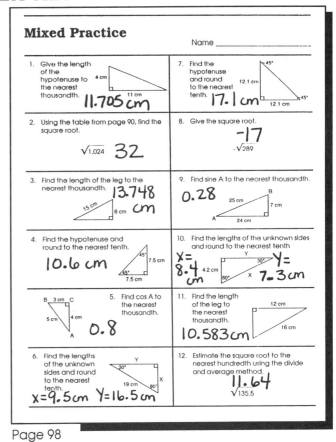

Mixed Practice

Name _____

1. Give the length of the hypotenuse to the nearest thousandth. **11.705 cm**

2. Using the table from page 90, find the square root. $\sqrt{1,024}$ **32**

3. Find the length of the leg to the nearest thousandth. **13.748 cm**

4. Find the hypotenuse and round to the nearest tenth. **10.6 cm**

5. Find cos A to the nearest thousandth. **0.8**

6. Find the lengths of the unknown sides and round to the nearest tenth. **x=9.5cm   Y=16.5cm**

7. Find the hypotenuse and round to the nearest tenth. **17.1 cm**

8. Give the square root. $-\sqrt{289}$ **-17**

9. Find sine A to the nearest thousandth. **0.28**

10. Find the lengths of the unknown sides and round to the nearest tenth **x= 8.4 cm   Y= 7.3 cm**

11. Find the length of the leg to the nearest thousandth. **10.583 cm**

12. Estimate the square root to the nearest hundredth using the divide and average method. $\sqrt{135.5}$ **11.64**

Page 98

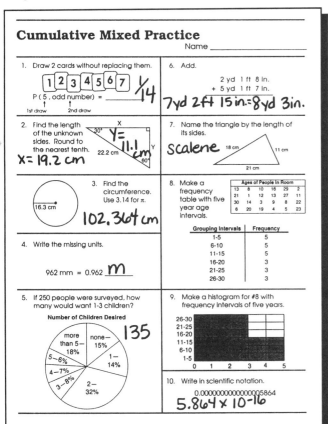

Cumulative Mixed Practice

Name _____

1. Draw 2 cards without replacing them.
   1 2 3 4 5 6 7 **1/14**
   P (5 , odd number) = ___
   1st draw   2nd draw

2. Find the length of the unknown sides. Round to the nearest tenth. **X= 19.2 cm   Y= 11.1 cm**

3. Find the circumference. Use 3.14 for π. **102.364 cm**

4. Write the missing units. 962 mm = 0.962 **m**

5. If 250 people were surveyed, how many would want 1-3 children? **135**

Number of Children Desired
more than 5— 18%, none— 15%, 1— 14%, 2— 32%, 3—8%, 4—7%, 5—6%

6. Add.
   2 yd 1 ft 8 in.
   + 5 yd 1 ft 7 in.
   7yd 2ft 15in.= 8yd 3in.

7. Name the triangle by the length of its sides. **scalene**

8. Make a frequency table with five year age intervals.

Ages of People in Room
13	8	10	16	29	2
21	1	12	13	27	11
30	14	3	9	8	22
6	20	19	4	5	23

Grouping Intervals	Frequency
1-5	5
6-10	5
11-15	5
16-20	3
21-25	3
26-30	3

9. Make a histogram for #8 with frequency intervals of five years.

10. Write in scientific notation.
0.0000000000000005864
5.864 x 10⁻¹⁶

Page 99

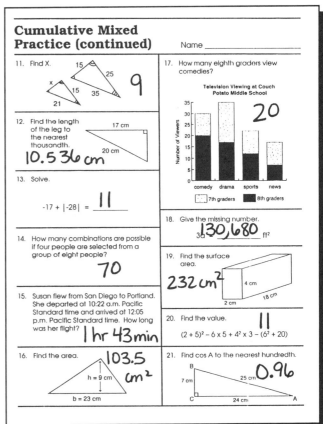

Cumulative Mixed Practice (continued)

Name _____

11. Find X. **9**

12. Find the length of the leg to the nearest thousandth. **10.536 cm**

13. Solve. -17 + |-28| = **11**

14. How many combinations are possible if four people are selected from a group of eight people? **70**

15. Susan flew from San Diego to Portland. She departed at 10:22 a.m. Pacific Standard time and arrived at 12:05 p.m. Pacific Standard time. How long was her flight? **1 hr 43 min**

16. Find the area. **103.5 cm²** h = 9 cm, b = 23 cm

17. How many eighth graders view comedies? **20**

Television Viewing at Couch Potato Middle School
(7th graders / 8th graders)
comedy drama sports news

18. Give the missing number. 3⁖ **130,680** ft²

19. Find the surface area. **232 cm²** 4 cm, 2 cm, 18 cm

20. Find the value. (2 + 5)² − 6 x 5 + 4² x 3 − (6² + 20) **11**

21. Find cos A to the nearest hundredth. **0.96** 7 cm, 25 cm, 24 cm

Page 100

©Instructional Fair, Inc.

ANSWER KEY

Cumulative Mixed Practice (continued)

Name _____

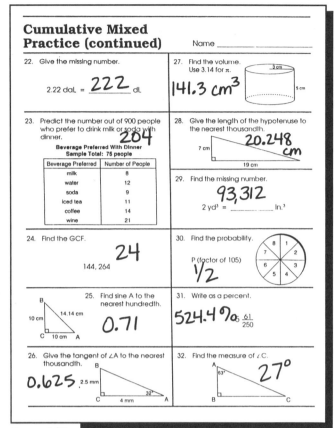

22. Give the missing number.

2.22 daL = **222** dL

27. Find the volume. Use 3.14 for π.

141.3 cm³

23. Predict the number out of 900 people who prefer to drink milk or soda with dinner. **204**

Beverage Preferred With Dinner
Sample Total: 75 people

Beverage Preferred	Number of People
milk	8
water	12
soda	9
iced tea	11
coffee	14
wine	21

28. Give the length of the hypotenuse to the nearest thousandth. **20.248 cm**

29. Find the missing number. **93,312**

2 yd³ = _____ in.³

24. Find the GCF. **24**

144, 264

30. Find the probability. **½**

P (factor of 105)

25. Find sine A to the nearest hundredth. **0.71**

26. Give the tangent of ∠A to the nearest thousandth. **0.625**

31. Write as a percent. **524.4 %** $\frac{61}{250}$

32. Find the measure of ∠C. **27°**

Page 101

Cumulative Mixed Practice (continued)

Name _____

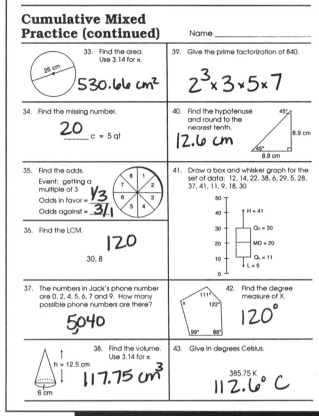

33. Find the area. Use 3.14 for π. **530.66 cm²**

39. Give the prime factorization of 840. **$2^3 \times 3 \times 5 \times 7$**

34. Find the missing number. **20** c = 5 qt

40. Find the hypotenuse and round to the nearest tenth. **12.6 cm**

35. Find the odds. Event: getting a multiple of 3
Odds in favor = **1/3**
Odds against = **3/1**

41. Draw a box and whisker graph for the set of data: 12, 14, 22, 38, 6, 29, 5, 28, 37, 41, 11, 9, 18, 30

H = 41
Qu = 30
MD = 20
QL = 11
L = 5

36. Find the LCM. **120**

30, 8

37. The numbers in Jack's phone number are 0, 2, 4, 5, 6, 7 and 9. How many possible phone numbers are there? **5,040**

42. Find the degree measure of X. **120°**

38. Find the volume. Use 3.14 for π. h = 12.5 cm **117.75 cm³**

43. Give in degrees Celsius. 385.75 K **112.6° C**

Page 102

About the Book ...

This book contains activity pages on such math topics as metric and customary units of measurement, triangles, tangent ratios, perimeter, area, probability, statistics, graphs, square roots, etc. A wide variety of approaches have been utilized whenever possible to stimulate interest and enhance motivation.

About the Author ...

Andrea Miles Moran lives in Connecticut with her husband and son, Miles. She received a Bachelor of Science degree from the University of Missouri-Columbia and a post baccalaureate teaching credential from San Diego State University. She taught junior high mathematics before moving to New York.

Credits ...

Author: Andrea Miles Moran
Artist: Tom Heggie
Project Director: Mina McMullin
Editor: Kathy Zaun
Graphic Design: Jill Kaufman
Production: Janie Schmidt
Cover Photo: ©Comstock, Inc. 1994
Cover Production: Annette Hollister-Papp